The CALL *to* CONTENTMENT

The

CALL

to

CONTENTMENT

Life Lessons from the Beatitudes

BY

NORMAN G. WILSON

AND

JERRY BRECHEISEN

WESLEYAN
PUBLISHING HOUSE
Indianapolis, Indiana

Special Thanks To—

Our wives, Nancy and Carol,
for their constant and loving support,
Don Cady and the staff at Wesleyan Publishing House
for their kind assistance, and Larry Wilson
for editorial insight and direction
in the preparation of this manuscript.

CONTENTS

Foreword   9

Introduction   11

1. Blessed Are the Poor in Spirit   15

2. Blessed Are Those Who Mourn   25

3. Blessed Are the Meek   35

4. Blessed Are Those Who Hunger and Thirst   47

5. Blessed Are the Merciful   57

6. Blessed Are the Pure in Heart   67

7. Blessed Are the Peacemakers   77

8. Blessed Are Those Who Are Persecuted   87

FOREWORD

I'm frequently asked where I learned the leadership principles that I have been privileged to share all over the world. My answer is simple: from the Bible. Every concept I teach has its basis in God's Word. My personal journey through its pages has not only enriched my life; it has given me insights into motivating others to pursue excellence.

Among the greatest of life lessons that I've discovered are those found in the Beatitudes. These peerless concepts for living and for leading form the introduction to Christ's Sermon on the Mount. Eight revolutionary and refreshing truths set the stage for the awe-inspiring words that follow, the heart of Jesus' teaching. No one has ever lived his or her ideals like the Master. And no one has ever been able to communicate those ideals in a more practical and yet powerful way.

This wisdom is desperately needed in these days! When many are searching for personal and corporate identity, when *who you are* is often judged by what you have or what you have done, when peace eludes the individual spirit as often as it does the human community, we're suddenly faced with calm and yet concrete answers. In these brief statements of truth and personal triumph called the Beatitudes, we see clearly how to climb without fear and walk without stumbling.

In my own spiritual development, I've learned the value of experiencing peace and contentment. No matter where I am, and no matter what I am called to do, I have found an inner assurance through personal faith. I have learned personally that I am not only called to excel, I am also called to enjoy the process. Jesus exemplified it. He is not only my Master, He is my Mentor. He traveled a road to contentment that leads through faith, forgiveness, meekness, and obedience. And it is a road that all who aspire to become something greater than what they are must travel.

Norm Wilson and Jerry Brecheisen are great communicators who have captured the heart of the Beatitudes and have applied their truths in understandable language. This book is a manual for anyone who has asked the question, *What matters most in my life?* The answer is as vital for personal contentment as it is for personal confidence.

JOHN C. MAXWELL

Founder, The INJOY Group
www.injoy.com

INTRODUCTION

Now when he saw the crowds, he went up on
a mountainside and sat down. His disciples came to him,
and he began to teach them. . . .
—Matthew 5:1–2

It was the traditional posture for a Jewish teacher. Seated,
surrounded by watchful eyes and eager ears. Also sitting
on the hard ground were devoted students who hoped
that the truths of the ages would fall from the lips of their
rabbi. They were attentive, expectant.

But this was no ordinary educator. This was the Master
whose words had echoed through the halls of heaven. And
these weren't merely the truths of the ages. They were the
truths of eternity. These were authoritative insights from One
who had lived a perfect life yet walked shoulder-to-shoulder
with the common man, life lessons from the Giver of Life.

There was no doubt that what He would say would be
worth enduring the discomfort of a Judean hillside to hear.
The God of Creation was about to school mere mortals on
the Kingdom of Heaven. He would show them how to be
whole and happy in the here and now while keeping the
gleam of eternity in their eyes. This would be no lifeless,
yawn-inspiring oration, but a refreshing draught from the
well of wisdom, welcome encouragement for world-weary
pilgrims. The disciples gathered; the crowds listened in.

We're still listening.

You and I need to know how to focus on the eternal.

We still need to learn contentment and love while living
in a world of grabbers and users. We still need blessing.
We still need peace. Perhaps now, more than ever.

The Secret to Happiness

Pascal said, "We never really live, but we hope to live," and it's true. Most of us are straining for something that seems just out of reach. Or else why are some people happy while others are steeped in misery? Why do some whistle while others whine?

What would it take to make you happy? A new job? A new home? A new relationship? Money in the bank? Better health? I've learned—often the hard way—that none of these things bring contentment. Oscar Wilde epitomized our condition when he wrote, "We are always arranging for being happy, but we never are."

Is it even possible to be content in a discontented world?

Jesus of Nazareth says yes.

In this awesome introduction to the world's greatest sermon, He spells out the winning formula in practical terms. Answers flowed from the heart of the Galilean that day as He defined happiness in a way that would cause any of us to sit patiently on the cold ground, eagerly awaiting the next word.

And the lesson was remarkably simple.

Jesus taught us that blessedness—happiness—isn't something you do or something you have or even something you are. Happiness is the response of your heart to the grace of God in your life. We are blessed—we are happy—because we have sought God and found Him. Happiness springs from knowing His peace and purpose in our lives.

The Real Thing

The Beatitudes form the beginning of Jesus' Sermon on the Mount. Matthew, the tax collector turned truth-gatherer, documented the event, recording the words of his Master. Here is the most practical job description for a human being that has ever been written. No greater life lessons have ever been taught.

Jesus began at the very center of human need—the longing for contentment. "Blessed are—," He pronounced. The phrase *blessed are* can be translated *happy are*.

The Greek language has two words for happiness. One indicates a happiness derived from external sources. The other, the one used here, denotes happiness that comes from within. The former draws joy from circumstances: good weather, good health, and good friends; possessions, position, and prestige.

That brand of happiness seldom brings lasting contentment. As Thackeray reflected, "*Vanity of Vanities!* which of us is happy in this world? Which of us has his desire? or, having it, is satisfied?"

The latter happiness exists even when the perks of prosperity are lacking. It is plugged into a different power source. Jesus says you can be refreshed even in the desert. You can sing even in the storm. You can learn to wrap your arms around a persecutor and call him friend.

That's not happiness as we usually understand it. It isn't happiness based on external conditions; it has an internal source. This is happiness that can be experienced regardless of the situation. It's the state of being that allowed the Apostle Paul to write from the confines of a Roman prison, "Rejoice in the Lord always. I will say it again: Rejoice!" (Phil. 4:4).

The Starting Point

It's said that the first word in the teaching of Buddha is *suffering*. I notice that the first word in the teaching of Christ is *blessed*. The Christian life is a life of blessing. Through these powerful principles, Jesus tells us how to live above the wanting, whining, and warring of society.

He tells us how to find comfort in the midst of pain.

He tells us how to feel joy in spite of grief.

He tells us how to feed on abundance though surrounded by poverty.

The Master Teacher says that we can be content without material things, holy without natural goodness, and loving without obvious graces.

Unnatural?

By whose standards?

Jesus set the bar high enough to make the leap humanly impossible, but low enough to make it attainable this side of heaven. Multitudes of hungry hearts departed the mountain filled with the Bread of Life.

The feast continues.

The Sermon on the Mount doesn't have an expiration date. The Beatitudes have an eternal shelf life. If you are seeking—really seeking, desperately seeking—a spiritual nail upon which to hang your tattered burdens, I invite you to begin here, with the Beatitudes.

Here are eight statements of eternal truth for times like these.

CHAPTER 1

*Blessed are the poor in spirit, for theirs is
the kingdom of heaven.*
—Matthew 5:3

"The whole world is on a mad quest for security and happiness," a French philosopher wrote. Few would disagree. Life is a constant whirl of activity, all intended to bring contentment. We seem convinced that if we can *have* enough or *be* enough or *do* enough, we'll be happy.

But happiness can be an elusive dream. As one Hollywood star commented, "I'm always searching for something that I can't find."

Full plates and three-car garages don't fill the aching void. It seems that the harder we try to be happy, the less happy we are. And whenever happiness stops for a visit, something inevitably appears to chase it away. One survey indicated that Americans don't think they get enough hugs. Of twenty thousand polled, 98 percent wanted to be hugged and touched more.

There's always some reason why we cannot be happy.

The Elusive Dream

Chasing happiness is a bit like trying to capture a butterfly. One boy observed a brightly colored lepidopteran flitting across the backyard. He watched in fascination as the beautiful creature moved weightlessly from flower to flower. *I must have it,* he thought. *My own butterfly!*

Abandoning a pile of toys—which only moments ago had been a source of contentment—the lad began to chase. Each time he inched near, some instinct seemed to warn the butterfly, and it skipped away. The harder he pursued, the faster the butterfly flew. Though never far away, it was always out of reach.

But the little fellow was determined. With a mighty effort he made one desperate, final lunge and grabbed it. Eagerly his little fingers squeezed the long-sought prize.

At last! he said to himself, *It's mine.*

But opening his fist, the child discovered that he held not the delicate creature he had been chasing, only its crushed remains.

Perhaps your own search for happiness has been like that. Contentment dangles just out of reach, only one inch—or one achievement, or one possession, or one relationship—away. Even as you grasp it, it evades you.

It's Never Enough

Someone asked financier John D. Rockefeller how much money was enough. "Just a little more," he answered, "Just a little more." Many are seeking that "little more" and finding that it's never enough.

Some seek happiness in a relationship. They're convinced that a certain marriage partner—or a new marriage partner—will bring happiness. They seek an "altar ego," someone with whom to live happily ever after. But too often, the wedding bells fall out of tune, and *Here Comes the Bride* becomes a haunting melody.

Others wander from one relationship to the next with the media-driven image of an ideal partner planted firmly in their minds. They try to fill the emotional void with an illicit affair, and then another. But instead of a time-share in Utopia, they find that they've purchased only broken dreams.

Still others seek happiness in mind-altering substances. Alcohol and other recreational drugs may make for a great evening, but there's always a morning after.

Bruised lives.

Wrecked relationships.

Lost jobs.

Addictions.

In place of happiness, the searchers find despair.

Sigmund Freud said that the chief duty of a human being is to endure life, and many are doing just that. They grit their teeth and hold on like passengers on an endless subway ride. One weary day drags into the next, and the night offers no relief.

It Is Real

But some people really are happy. They don't endure life, they enjoy it. They grab every day like a Christmas present from under the tree and shake it with wonder. For them, each sunrise is a sacred invocation, and every sunset a peaceful benediction. Life is a symphony with Jesus as conductor.

A man on an airplane was seated next to a machinery manufacturer. He asked the industrialist, "How do you know when you've produced the perfect machine?"

"That's easy," the fellow answered. "When a machine is running just the way it should, it sings. Listen to the engines on this plane. Can't you hear them singing?"

People are the same.

When they're running right—when they're in tune with God, their neighbors, and themselves—their lives sing. Perhaps that's why Paul said, "Speak to one another with psalms, hymns and spiritual songs. Sing and make music in your heart to the Lord . . ." (Eph. 5:19).

It's true that some people don't have a lot to sing about. They are victims of life's assault and battery. But the fact is, you *can* be happy in spite of it all.

The Poor in Spirit

Abraham Lincoln was convinced that most people are about as happy as they make up their minds to be. He saw happiness as a decision, an act of the will grounded in the grace of God.

We often think, *I'll be happy if I get this . . . go there . . . find that . . . become this.* Yet many have been there and done that (and bought the T-shirt), and they're still unhappy. That's because happiness does not have its source outside the self. It's rooted in the soul.

There is more to you than what looks back from the mirror. Human beings are composed of both body and spirit. The spirit is the inner self. The word *spirit* suggests *breath.* God breathed into man's nostrils the breath of life. The real you is on the inside, and that's the one who needs to be content.

It's a Right Attitude

Much of modern religion is focused on external things—doing this or that, or not doing this or that. But you can do (or not do) a hundred things and still be light years away from the Kingdom. The Bible says that man looks on the outward appearance, but God looks on the heart. The Pharisees shouted, Look at me! God says, Look *to* me.

Genuine happiness results from having a correct attitude of spirit.

On the control panel of an airplane there is an instrument that tells the pilot whether the plane is level. It indicates the plane's *attitude.* Another dial refers to the *altitude* of the plane—its height above the earth. Being poor in spirit has to do with attitude, not altitude. It is having a right orientation toward God.

D. L. Moody adds, "One of the strongest signs that a man is growing in grace, is that he is growing smaller and Christ is growing larger." The poor in spirit don't disparage themselves; they exalt Christ.

It's a Proper Self-Image

In an interesting study, one hundred people were handed a pen and a blank piece of paper. Ninety-seven of them proceeded to write their own name on the paper, perhaps indicating what was first on their mind. Awhile back, Herbert B. Wolfeschlegelsteinhausenbergerendorff of Philadelphia complained that the newspaper had left the "u" out of his name. Some people can see nothing but themselves in any situation.

The beginning of contentment is not self-abasement, but it's not self-aggrandizement either. You may think you have everything under control—even the newspaper. But "world controllers" don't meet the height requirement set by Jesus. He said the blessed (happy, contented) people are those who depend on a higher source than themselves.

The poor in spirit understand their *needs* as well as their *niceties*. They see themselves and their Maker clearly—and they know who's who!

But don't get the wrong idea. To me, poverty of spirit is not fear of success or clinging to the bottom rung of life's ladder. God has a higher view of you and me.

David, the songwriter of the Old Testament, had 20/20 vision about himself. He wrote, "I praise you because I am fearfully and wonderfully made; your works are wonderful, I know that full well" (Ps. 139:14).

Being poor in spirit means seeing yourself clearly, as God does. It means being humble before Him, yet confident, as one of His prized possessions.

It's a Royal Birth

There's a line from a Gilbert and Sullivan opera that characterizes our attitude about self:

> If you wish in the world to advance,
>   Your merits, your bound to enhance,
> You must stir it and stump it,
>   And blow your own trumpet,
> Or trust me, you haven't a chance.

But that trumped-up self-worth is contrary to this beatitude. Your real value comes from your relationship to God.

God created you.

Satan claimed you.

And Christ paid the price to buy you back.

You may have so much blue-blood in you that you'd have to add red dye to get a blood count, but that doesn't make you royalty. Royal blood comes from royal birth, or rather *re*birth—being born supernaturally into the family of the King, Jesus Christ. Only when His blood flows through your spiritual veins are you listed in the registry of heaven. And only then can you enjoy the contentment of a right relationship to God.

A royal birth?

It is possible. We can be born from above—totally apart from our own efforts at self-advancement. The Scripture says, "He saved us, not because of righteous things we had done, but because of his mercy. He saved us through the washing of rebirth and renewal by the Holy Spirit . . ." (Titus 3:5).

So what does it mean to be poor in spirit?

It means to be personally destitute of any plans to

impress God or sneak into His heaven. It means to depend totally on Him for holiness, wholeness, and happiness. It means to be born again into God's royal family.

Does that describe you?

Destination Heaven

The poor in spirit aren't underprivileged, of course. The point of Jesus' teaching, in fact, is that they are blessed. They have lots to be happy about and plenty to look forward to. One popular songwriter said, "It's hip to be square." If so, it's also cool to be poor!

The poor in spirit have a good thing coming.

Happiness Is a Confirmed Reservation

When I'm traveling and need hotel accommodations, I call a toll-free number and secure a room with my credit card. The operator gives me a confirmation number. Hurriedly I write it on the edge of a map or scribble it on a napkin. That number is seldom needed, but there is security in knowing that I have it. I have a confirmed reservation.

So do the poor in spirit.

"Happy are the poor in spirit," Jesus said, "for theirs is the kingdom of heaven." In other words, they can be happy because they have a guaranteed reservation. They know where they are going.

A man raced through the airport to catch his flight. He passed through security in record time and reached the gate with only moments to spare. Hurrying aboard the aircraft, he found his seat, opened his laptop computer, and tried to work. But his mind was awhirl from the constant pressure of work and travel.

A few moments later, another passenger boarded the plane and took the empty seat next to the harried traveler.

Buckling his seatbelt, the newcomer turned to his neighbor and asked, "Where are you headed?"

The man looked up from his laptop, his mind still on some last-minute task. His face went blank. "Where am I going?" he wondered aloud. "Which trip is this?" A brief but embarrassing silence was broken when he asked, "Where is this plane going?"

"Denver," the fellow passenger responded.

"Well, that's where I'm going!"

He had a ticket. He was buckled into the cabin of a state-of-the-art airplane worth several million dollars. He was going somewhere in a hurry, but he didn't know where.

Many people are unhappy because their lives have no direction, no purpose, no goal. They don't know where they are going. They're on a merry-go-round that's had brake failure. Trapped in place, they go round and round in the same circles. They work to make more money, to buy more things, so they can enjoy more pleasures—all costing more money. You've heard it said that the world makes way for a man who knows where he's going. That may be because there are so few of them!

Runaways are a fact of modern life. Bored, listless, restless and unhappy, people drop their responsibilities in a pile and strike out for parts unknown. What is most disturbing is not what they are running from, but what they are running to—nothing.

Jesus said that the poor in spirit are happy. And they have reason to be. They know where they are going.

Check, Please

For each of us, the merry-go-round will end someday. What then? What happens when you check out of life?

Prior to his death from cancer, former Beatle George Harrison left a note for family and friends, indicating that he was on a continual search for God. To him, life was cyclical, and death was simply another chapter in the search.

But Jesus spoke of life as linear—those who put their faith in Him are bound for a destination. You can know that your ultimate destination is heaven, and that knowledge is a source of true happiness.

We live in an age of uncertainty.

People are concerned about the events that are shaping history. Where are we going? What is happening to our world? Governments rise and fall. Leaders climb to power only to be toppled by the ambitions of others. Armaments proliferate, and the potential for world destruction has been a reality for many years. We can't be sure what will happen from one day to the next.

But there's no need to feel insecure about your future.

God has written the last chapter of your life. The Bible tells us that everything will change one day—for the better. Second Peter 3:10: "The heavens will disappear with a roar; the elements will be destroyed by fire, and the earth and everything in it will be laid bare."

That's not a recipe for disaster; it's the announcement of a victory party. The annihilation of the earth is the inauguration of heaven on earth. Peter writes, "But in keeping with his promise we are looking forward to a new heaven and a new earth, the home of righteousness" (2 Pet. 3:13).

The poor in spirit have that hope, expressed in a classic gospel song:

> O Lord, you know,
>   I have no friend like you,
> If heaven's not my home
>   then Lord what will I do?
> The angels beckon me

from heaven's open door,
And I can't feel at home
in this world anymore.

Jesus said, "Do not let your hearts be troubled. Trust in God; trust also in me. In my Father's house are many rooms; if it were not so, I would have told you. I am going there to prepare a place for you. And if I go and prepare a place for you, I will come back and take you to be with me that you also may be where I am" (John 14:1–3).

Heaven is not a state of mind. Heaven is an address, a real place, inhabited by real people—the poor in spirit. These are people who have taken their focus off of themselves and placed their hope in Jesus Christ, people who know where they are going. People like you?

Blessed are the poor in spirit, for theirs is the kingdom of heaven.

———————————

Jesus promised a Kingdom to come, but our blessings aren't just futuristic. The next beatitude shows how we can find comfort in spite of real-world ills.

CHAPTER 2

Blessed are those who mourn,
for they will be comforted.
—Matthew 5:4

I f you've ever done door-to-door sales or church visitation, you know that it's possible to spend a lot of time standing at the wrong door. It's been my experience that the most obvious entrance to a house is usually the one with the entertainment center on the other side. And the "right" door is usually around the corner next to the satellite dish and past the discriminating German shepherd.

The Beatitudes seem at first to be the wrong door.

They stand in stark contrast to popular sentiment. Jesus' message was diametrically opposed to that of the religious elitists of His day. Theirs was a message of religion by works. They were comforted only by the result of their latest effort. And when their physical strength waned or their alms ran low, their hopes for receiving God's blessing dimmed.

A New Testament writer addressed that penchant for seeking salvation by works, which goes all the way back to the Old Testament. Then he reminded us of someone, a godly man named Abraham, who lived outside the box. Romans 4:2–5:

> If, in fact, Abraham was justified by works, he had something to boast about—but not before God. What does the Scripture say? "Abraham believed God, and it was credited to him as righteousness."

Now when a man works, his wages are not credited to him as a gift, but as an obligation. However, to the man who does not work but trusts God who justifies the wicked, his faith is credited as righteousness.

Jesus' uplifting message contrasted with the depressing message of the Pharisees. Heaven's forgiveness is the answer for earth's folly.

Here's the secret: happiness doesn't result from what you do. Happiness comes by staking your claim on what God has already done for you.

Godly Sorrow

The Pharisees had about as much spiritual enthusiasm as night watchmen at a coffin factory. They delighted in tying chains of ritual around the legs of the faithful, then hollering *Fire!*

Jesus put the fire out before it started. His message was like a cool refreshing stream. Bring me the sorrow for your past, and I will give you a hope for the future, He offered. They had nothing else to bring. It was their sorrow or nothing.

Godly Sorrow Includes Repentance

This isn't the sorrow that accompanies the loss of a loved one or friend. It's much more that that. It's a sorrow of the spirit, an emotional embarrassment that results from living life without reference to God. The Bible calls it godly sorrow, and it's the beginning of a life-giving formula: sorrow plus repentance equals salvation. "Godly sorrow brings repentance that leads to salvation and leaves no regret, but worldly sorrow brings death" (2 Cor. 7:10).

Notice that repentance is the link.

Sorrow plus repentance equals salvation. Sorrow alone

won't do. It must be joined by repentance. That includes volition—an act of the will. Godly sorrow is an attitude of the mind and heart that turns from disobedience *against* God toward deliverance *by* God.

Saying "I'm sorry!" isn't enough. That doesn't constitute mourning. Mourning is more reflective, more contemplative. "I'm *so* sorry!" is closer, but not close enough to win a horse-shoe throwing contest.

"I'm sorry enough to—"

Ringer!

Godly sorrow is a deep spiritual mourning that produces a change of heart. It results in changed behavior. That brings inner happiness—contentment— because our sorrow is met by God's supply.

When we become sorry for what we are, God makes us something better.

Godly Sorrow Brings Forgiveness

A therapist will tell you that the first step toward recovery from any problem is to admit that recovery is necessary.

And my first step in receiving the spiritual comfort of the Lord Jesus Christ is to admit that I can't get along without it.

We live in a world that can turn on a television set from across the room but can't find a way to extend a hand across the chasm between God and humanity.

What's the problem?

Literary giant G. K. Chesterton responded to a newspaper reader's question with an interesting insight. "Dear Mr. Chesterton," the reader began, "What's wrong with the world today?"

Chesterton's reply: "Dear Sir, I am."

The comfort of God's forgiveness belongs to those who admit they have a problem, to those who mourn their sin.

Psalm 32:1–2, "Blessed is he whose transgressions are forgiven, whose sins are covered. Blessed is the man whose sin the Lord does not count against him and in whose spirit is no deceit."

Feels So Good

The word *comfort* is beautiful in its original language. It is a combination of two Greek words meaning *call* and *near.*

To call near.

That's exemplified beautifully in Jesus' calling the little children near and blessing them (Matt. 19:14), and it culminates in the greatest invitation of all time: "Come to me, all you who are weary and burdened, and I will give you rest" (Matt. 11:28). In this beatitude, Jesus calls mourners near and comforts them with His grace. Spiritual happiness— blessedness—is the result.

We Have Hope

Charles Schultz's legendary cartoon figure Linus was known for carrying a security blanket. No matter what the situation, Linus could face it if he had his personal comforter. His immortal line: "Happiness is a warm blanket."

No matter how young or old we are, sometimes we need a security blanket. We mourn, and we need the security of hope. Christianity doesn't deny the stark realities of life. Just look at its most recognizable symbol, the Cross! It's the emblem, as the beloved hymn says, of suffering and shame. All of the tragedy, anguish, injustice, and suffering of human existence are wrapped up in that old, rugged cross. And by taking that cross—by giving His life on it—Jesus Christ provided the greatest source of hope available to the human heart.

Paul puts it this way: "And he is the head of the body, the

church; he is the beginning and the firstborn from among the dead, so that in everything he might have the supremacy. For God was pleased to have all his fullness dwell in him, and through him to reconcile to himself all things, whether things on earth or things in heaven, by making peace through his blood, shed on the cross" (Col. 1:18–20).

The physical and emotional sorrow of the Cross resulted in your spiritual comfort. Even in a time of mourning, you can be happy.

Why?

Because Jesus provides hope.

Paul the apostle understood that. He had an obvious source of comfort when he wrote, "We are hard pressed on every side, but not crushed; perplexed, but not in despair; persecuted, but not abandoned; struck down, but not destroyed" (2 Cor. 4:8–9).

Having endured beatings, shipwrecks, stoning, imprisonment, hunger and thirst, and dangers of every description for the cause of the gospel, Paul could call all of them "light afflictions" (2 Cor. 4:8).

Why?

Because they weren't worthy of being compared with the glory that would later be revealed.

He advised, "We do not want you to be ignorant about those who fall asleep, or to grieve like the rest of men, who have no hope" (1 Thess. 4:13).

Many misinterpret that counsel, taking it to mean that Christians never have sorrow. But Paul didn't say that. He didn't say that I would never weep. Even Jesus wept. You and I are without sin or shame when we weep for the sorrows of this world.

There is a glory yet to be revealed, a hope beyond the grave. We have hope beyond our present situation.

We're Not Alone

When Jesus spoke to His disciples near the end of His earthly ministry, He gave them a promise. They were heartsick that they would no longer walk the roads of life with their beloved friend and mentor; His words were heartwarming and helpful. "And I will pray the Father, and he shall give you another Comforter, that he may abide with you for ever . . ." (John 14:16).

"Another Comforter"—another friend and mentor.

Remember that a comforter is one who is called alongside to help. In other words, Jesus was saying, I will not leave you alone like a street orphan to fend for yourself. I will send someone to stand alongside you in every situation of life. During every long night, through every frightening circumstance, the Comforter will be with you.

And this promise isn't exclusive to the Twelve! It's ours as well.

I know what a comfort the presence of a friend or loved one can be in time of trouble. (That is why the Bible admonishes Christians to weep with those who weep, as well as to rejoice with those who rejoice.) Many stay away at a time of setback or sorrow because they don't know what to say. It may be *presence* that is needed most.

There's a classic example.

A group of Christian educators was invited to Russia to teach ethics and moral values in government-run institutions. Two of the educators were assigned to an orphanage. It was the Christmas season, and the teachers were given the privilege of telling the story of Jesus' birth to children who had never heard it.

Realizing that this was a marvelous opportunity, the teachers gathered the orphan children in a cold classroom and told the story in great detail—the glorious announcement, the arduous journey to Bethlehem, and the birth of the Messiah in the manger. The children listened carefully. Their eyes widened in excitement as the teacher told of angel songs filling the night air and Magi bringing gifts to the baby.

To reinforce the story, the educators distributed bits of cardboard to the children and asked them each to make a tiny manger. The teachers also provided small pieces of cloth and wrapping paper, and through their interpreter, instructed the children to make a doll representing the baby Jesus.

One of the teachers noticed an orphan boy meticulously arranging the items to form the manger scene as he envisioned it. As the teacher came closer, she put her hand on the boy's shoulder and bent to look into the crude manger. Inside were two pieces of wrapping paper fashioned into dolls. With the help of her interpreter, she asked the boy why there were two babies in the manger crib.

Childlike wonder took over as the child embellished the story he had just heard for the first time. "Well, I was visiting them that night," he began. "And when baby Jesus' momma laid Him in the crib, He looked right over at me and said, 'Do you have a place to stay tonight?' I said, 'No, baby Jesus. I don't have a momma and poppa.'"

As the boy continued his story, he kept his eyes lowered and slowly traced the little nativity scene with his finger. "Then baby Jesus said, 'That's all right. You can stay with me.'" The boy's eyes were never lifted. "'But where would I stay?' I asked Him. And he patted the straw and told me, 'You can stay right here beside me.'"

Suddenly the shy child picked up the wrapping-paper baby and acted out the scene. "So I climbed up into the crib and lay down beside Him. He stretched his arm across my chest and went to sleep. Pretty soon we were both asleep, me and Jesus in that crib."

Barely able to see through her tears, the teacher watched as the boy's own tears welled up in his eyes like tiny pools. As he thought about the story, they soon spilled one by one onto his ruddy cheeks.

And the teacher knew why. This little Russian boy without a past or a future understood the gospel perfectly. Even if no one else cared about him, Jesus did.

Divine presence is real. We have a Comforter, the Holy Spirit.

We Have Resources

One of the pop interests of the twenty-first century is *geocaching*. A cache, comprising anything from a logbook to an item of jewelry, is encased in a plastic bag or covered bucket and hidden in a remote, outdoor location. Enthusiasts with hand-held computers use global positioning satellites (GPS) to calculate the exact longitude and latitude and locate the cache.

The psalmist David also had a GPS—a *God* Positioning System—which proved to be of greater value. Psalm 119:105, "Your word is a lamp to my feet and a light for my path."

Blessed (happy, contented) are those who mourn their dependence on self for life's direction, for they are comforted by God's guidance. You are not adrift in life; you have means of finding your way.

The Bible.

Prayer.

The counsel of other Christians.

The spoken word.

A song.

God has given you Spirit-led and Spirit-anointed

resources for finding your way through the busy streets and intersections of life.

We Have Eternal Comfort

Those who have mourned the need for earth's affirmations will discover a final and eternal comfort: heaven.

You've seen it a hundred times. The toddler trips over a coffee table or some other object and falls down. A painful cry erupts from the tiny one. A parent rushes to the point of need, picks up the child, and comforts the hurt away. "There, there," Mama says. "You're all right. I've got you—you'll be all right." With a hug and a reassuring word, the crying is stopped.

That's a preview of heaven.

One day the Lord will pick us up from the painful places of this life, and we will hear in tones unmatched by any earthly parent, "You're all right. I've got you—you'll be all right."

And we will be—for all eternity.

John 16:20–22: "I tell you the truth, you will weep and mourn while the world rejoices. You will grieve, but your grief will turn to joy. A woman giving birth to a child has pain because her time has come; but when her baby is born she forgets the anguish because of her joy that a child is born into the world. So with you: Now is your time of grief, but I will see you again and you will rejoice, and no one will take away your joy."

Happy Here and Now

I heard of a newspaper columnist who asked people what were the happiest ten years of their lives. Some said it was the time between the ages of twenty and thirty, when their children were babies and life's major problems had not yet started. Others responded that it was the decade between thirty and forty, when as husband and wife they dealt together with daily dilemmas and looked forward to the future.

Interestingly, many said that their happiest time is now. One lady wrote, "I thought the best ten years were from thirty to forty, then forty to fifty. But it just kept getting better. Now I am seventy; ask me again in ten years."

Another man—in his nineties—was heard to say, "No complaints. I am happy in the Lord and looking forward to what God has in store."

Happiness is not freedom from pressure or pain, and contentment isn't the absence of sorrow. In fact, as Jesus said, you can be happy even when you mourn, because in your mourning you will be comforted.

———————

Are you in the market for real estate? Hold off on that purchase. The next beatitude promises an inheritance that'll knock your socks off!

CHAPTER 3

Blessed are the meek,
for they will inherit the earth.
—Matthew 5:5

A
s I child I played the game that went something like this: interlocking my fingers, I would whisper, "This is the church and this is the steeple; open the doors and see all the people."

Understanding this beatitude is like opening the doors and seeing the people of God for the first time. It mirrors both the character of the Christ and the characteristic of the Christian.

Blessed (happy, contented) are the meek. Blessed are those who have discovered the joy of surrendering the details of their lives to God.

We live in an anxious world, filled with countless details. Winston Churchill commented that our anxieties are so many that "one cancels out another."

Not quite.

Our moods can be like the weather—partly cloudy or partly sunny depending on the dynamics of the day. But almost certainly, one of those moods will be worry. Henry Ward Beecher said that worry is like rust upon the blade. We've all felt the rust of worry, grinding against the smooth flow of our lives.

This beatitude addresses the problem of anxiety and reminds every Christian that there is a solution. Happy are those who have traded their tension for trust, for they shall inherit the peace of God.

They shall inherit.

That's not some pie-in-the-sky promise. It's a bread-on-the-table offer, a present-tense reality. To those of Jesus' day, traveling legalistic highways mapped by the religious elite, it was a welcome exit ramp. Jesus took His listeners back to the refuge of the Psalms:

> Do not fret because of evil men
>> or be envious of those who do wrong;
> for like the grass they will soon wither,
>> like green plants they will soon die away.
> Trust in the Lord and do good;
>> dwell in the land and enjoy safe pasture.
> Delight yourself in the Lord
>> and he will give you the desires of your heart.
> —Psalm 37:1–4

A mechanic and a heart surgeon were having a conversation. Both were bragging about their professions. The mechanic said to the surgeon, "I say the work we mechanics do is just as complicated as yours."

The surgeon wisely replied, "Maybe so, but let me see you work on an engine while it's still running!"

The third beatitude is a promise to those whose engines are still running—running with the pounding pace of a society that worries about the future, yet lives as if there isn't one. To them, it promises peace.

For the Meek Only

I heard about a spoiled nephew who was expecting an inheritance from his well-to-do uncle. The attorney read the will while relatives waited and the nephew squirmed in the office chair, planning his expenditures. Finally, the big moment arrived.

"And to my nephew, Jack—"

Happy tension filled the nephew's heart.

"To my nephew, Jack, I just want to say Hi!"

Have you thought that life isn't fair? The will was read, and all you got was a personal greeting? Perhaps the blatant inequities of life have made you more than a little angry. The rich get richer and the poor get poorer, and it seems that the gap is ever widening. There seems to be no correlation between a man's worth and his wealth, and many people are disturbed by it.

Taking Care of Number One was a best selling book—and many people still live by that slogan.

"You have to assert yourself."

"The Lord helps those who help themselves."

"If you don't take it, no one will give it to you."

For some, it's as if the first sound they heard at birth was the starting gun for the rat race! They spend their lives clawing, scratching, climbing, and fighting to get all they can.

In contrast, Jesus said the meek will win out—without leaving a scratch.

William Carey, the "father of modern missions," wouldn't be considered a great success by twenty-first century standards. He didn't have a best-selling book. He didn't have a television ministry. He didn't have a speaker's bureau making appointments for his public appearances. Carey wasn't considered a good preacher, and he was turned down for ordination by his church. As a missionary to India, he went for nearly ten years without making a single convert.

Pretty meek by today's standards.

But William Carey had a heart for God and a burden for souls. He made a mark that every other missionary of the gospel has aimed for. He was faithful.

Blessed are the meek—the faithful in spite of fame or fortune—for they are enjoying the "advance" on their inheritance.

What do I have to do to experience that kind of life?

The Surrender That Leads to Victory

The Greek word translated *meek* suggests *gentle* or *trusting*. Blessed are those who gently trust their Lord. It doesn't say, "Blessed are the wimps," however. It means blessed are those who quietly surrender to God.

We're Trapped by Ambition

The Scriptures describe two approaches to spirituality. Let's call them spiritual Type A and spiritual Type B. The Type A person is in charge—spiritually and otherwise. He or she is directing life's symphony—and usually playing first violin as well! Clinging to control, the spiritual Type A resents takeover attempts by anyone—including God!

The result is emotional and spiritual anxiety.

Paul describes that mental state: "The sinful mind is hostile to God. It does not submit to God's law, nor can it do so" (Rom. 8:7). Since *self* is in control instead of God, there is a natural hostility to His will and to His way.

"It does not submit to God's law, nor can it do so."

Trapped!

The person who is driving under the influence of self is trapped in life's fast lane—the lane that leads to a certain crash. James 1:14–15: "Each one is tempted when, by his own evil desire, he is dragged away and enticed. Then, after desire has conceived, it gives birth to sin; and sin, when it is full-grown, gives birth to death."

We're Set Free by Surrender

In contrast, the spiritually Type B person has surrendered the wheel to another. Some of the better advice that the Old Testament character Job received was to do just that—surrender. Job 22:21: "Submit to God and be at peace with him; in this way prosperity will come to you."

I've found that I can be at peace in the turmoil of these times. How? By surrendering. That means laying down not only my "arms," but also my "harms"—placing my fears as well as my faith into God's hands. Romans 8:6: "The mind of sinful man is death, but the mind controlled by the Spirit is life and peace. . . ."

Give up without a Fight

You've probably seen news broadcasts of hostage situations. Happily, the end is peaceful most of the time. The reporter often says of an apprehended culprit, "He gave up without a struggle."

Spiritual meekness means giving up to God "without a struggle." Jesus epitomized that attitude in Matthew 11:29: "Take my yoke upon you and learn from me, for I am gentle and humble in heart. . . ."

Jesus' life was one of complete surrender to His heavenly Father's will.

That was seen in His conscious act of surrender to the Cross. In the Garden of Gethsemane, He looked into the cup of death and saw the agonized end of His life—the sinless one suffering in the place of every sinner. His humanity begged to be spared. But this was Father's plan, and from the earliest days of Jesus' life, it was evident that Father's business was His business.

Matthew records, "He fell with his face to the ground and prayed, 'My Father, if it is possible, may this cup be taken from me. Yet not as I will, but as you will'" (Matt. 26:39).

The inheritance of happiness comes only after fully surrendering to the heavenly Father's plan.

You can make a full surrender. You can wave the white flag over the rampart of works. And here's the difference between man's kingdom and God's: Once you surrender—once you declare your spiritual dependence on God—you won't be taken prisoner. You'll be set free! You'll receive the inheritance, forevermore.

The Reading of the Will

God doesn't keep His gold reserves locked in some unknown vault. They're on the bottom shelf, where anyone can reach them.

A little boy went to the store with his grandfather. Grandpa put one quarter in the M&M's machine in the lobby—and then another, until he had filled his cupped hands with the multi-colored candies. "Here, Son," the grandfather said, "Let me pour these into your hands." But the grandson refused.

"No, sir!" the boy protested. "You're hands are bigger than mine. They'll spill all over the floor!"

How often have we refused handfuls of God's grace, thinking that somehow God is too big or too far away to whisper the extravagant promises of His supply to our tiny spirits? Jesus said we will inherit *the earth,* not lot #1735 in North township!

This grand inheritance is ours to enjoy.

We Inherit Blessings

First, the meek will inherit the blessings of the earth. The spiritually Type A—the self-directed, worried, and anxious—

miss out on earth's blessings. They miss the sweet aromas of life, like the scent of a gently perspiring field of daisies exercising in the midday air; the blossoming rose; rain-covered grass.

They also miss spectacular sights, such as Jesus painting a morning sky on the canvas of the night; the teasing smile of the toddler; a lover's gaze.

Spiritually Type A people even miss the awesome sounds, like the symphony of the brook tumbling over mischievous rocks; the hopeful flapping of a mourning dove's wings; the autumn wind singing a wintry lullaby to a pine.

One wrote:

> The little cares that fretted me,
>   I lost them yesterday,
> Among the fields above the sea,
>   among the winds at play,
> Among the lowing of the herds,
>   the rustling of the trees,
> Among the singing of the birds,
>   the humming of the bees;
> The foolish fears of what might pass,
>   I cast them all away,
> Among the clover scented grass,
>   among the new mowed hay,
> Among the rustling of the corn,
>   where drowsy poppies nod,
> Where ill-thoughts die and good are born,
>   out in the fields of God.
>   —Unknown

We Inherit the Promise

The meek inherit the promise of the earth also. Planet earth is scheduled for God's reconstructive surgery. Its barrenness will be changed to beauty, its toil to triumph, its hardship to "Hallelujah!" Romans 8:20–21: "For the creation was subjected to frustration, not by its own choice, but by the will of the one who subjected it, in hope that the creation itself will be liberated from its bondage to decay and brought into the glorious freedom of the children of God."

Heaven is not a rehab ward for strugglers (the spiritually Type A). It is a place of rest for the peaceful (the spiritually Type B), who have inherited the promises of God. Like Abraham walking around the land of God's promise and claiming every inch of it by faith, the Christ-controlled person can pace off the promises of God and drive a stake of faith in each one.

Strength for weariness.

Holiness for humanness.

Peace for brokenness.

Power for weakness.

Child of God, it's all yours—and more! You have been made heir to eternal blessings.

An Inheritance of Joy

Many have found the inheritance of a fortune to be anything but joyous. In fact, it can be deadly.

Years ago, I read of a woman living in a large metropolitan area who had inherited a fortune. Some time later she was found murdered in her home. When police searched the house, they found thousands of dollars hidden in garbage cans and various other places. Even so, her murderers had stolen millions.

It was discovered that this unfortunate woman had lived a lonely and tragic existence. She didn't trust banks, so she kept all her money at home. Alone and afraid, she was a prisoner of her wealth until the day she was murdered for it.

Perhaps Andrew Carnegie, the great industrialist and philanthropist, was right when he said, "Millionaires who laugh are rare, very rare indeed."

But in His message on happiness, Jesus included those with a rich inheritance. He said, "Happy are the meek, for they will inherit the earth."

There's Joy in Receiving

This inheritance is a gift, not something you must earn. You simply receive what's coming to you by virtue of your birth—your spiritual birth.

Romans 8:16–17: "The Spirit himself testifies with our spirit that we are God's children. Now if we are children, then we are heirs—heirs of God and co-heirs with Christ, if indeed we share in his sufferings in order that we may also share in his glory."

Sometimes those who inherit are not the children of the deceased. The beneficiary may be someone who worked for the benefactor, perhaps a faithful employee. Some leave large inheritances to pets. (There are several millionaire cats living on planet earth!)

But the inheritance that Jesus promises is reserved for members of the family—God's family.

Paul specified that in his letter to the Galatians: "So you are no longer a slave, but a son; and since you are a son, God has made you also an heir" (4:7).

There's Joy in Security

An inheritance brings security. You can just rest in the rest of it!

It is the nature of a loving father to do all He can for His children. And God has done precisely that. He has not only provided life itself, but an abundant inheritance as well. Through faith, we are joint heirs with His Son, the Lord Jesus Christ. Whatever Christ receives from God, His father, we, too, will receive!

Often, when a child inherits money, it is placed in a trust fund, some to provide for education, and some for living expenses and other needs. The concern is that the young person might not have the aptitude for managing wealth. It may be squandered or wasted, and before long there might be nothing left.

But ours is an inexhaustible inheritance—and we get it now as well as in the future!

On April 14, 2000, Wall Street suffered the biggest one-day fall in history. U.S. markets lost an estimated \$2 trillion. Bill Gates, the chairman of Microsoft, saw his personal fortune drop some \$30 billion in a matter of hours. Even after that catastrophic loss, it is estimated that Mr. Gates was still worth more than forty-six billion dollars—that's \$46,000,000,000.

The average wage earner may find that amount of money inconceivable. But count the zeros. There are nine of them. And did you notice that after the nine zeros, there is a decimal point? That tiny dot means that even this enormous fortune has an ending point.

But the inheritance prepared for the children of God is inexhaustible. There is no decimal point. It will never end.

One of the American frontiersman said, "I have inherited nothing from my father but an old cap, a worn out pair of britches, and a tendency to rheumatism."

You have more.

The testimony of countless Christians has asserted the truth: happiness is not found in material things. Inheriting a fortune would not make you any happier than you are right now. But you can be happy by surrendering control of your life to God. For when the will of the Father is read, you will inherit the earth.

You can surrender the struggles of life for the promises of eternity. Blessed are the meek, for they will inherit the earth.

Can we be satisfied spiritually? The next beatitude gives the answer.

CHAPTER 4

Blessed are those who hunger and thirst for righteousness,
for they will be filled.
—Matthew 5:6

S ir Ernest Shackleton and his companions experienced extreme and continuous hunger on their polar expedition. When describing the experience, Shackleton said that they found it difficult to think about anything other than food or eating.

The fourth beatitude is for the spiritual Shackletons of the world, those who can think of nothing but their hunger for God.

It promises that they will be filled.

Jesus used hunger and thirst to characterize a passion for goodness—for spiritual rightness. This condition is a deep, insatiable craving, not something that can be satisfied by spiritual snack crackers and a soft drink. It describes a person who has gone without food and water for an extended period of time. Every fiber of his being cries out for nourishment.

Jesus didn't say that if you seek *happiness* you will be satisfied. Too many hunger and thirst for anything but righteousness. The gains and glories of the world captivate and control them. What Jesus did say is that if you seek *righteousness*, you will be *happy*. Most people have the proverbial cart before the horse. Their mindset: When I have everything I want and need, when my business is established, when I've made my fortune and had my fun, then I'll seek God.

The Teacher, however, said that the subject of our search

must be righteousness—a right relationship with God. That implies reflecting all the holiness and goodness that make up the character of God.

When God created Adam in the garden paradise, the first man reflected God's righteousness. God put the stamp of His own image on that piece of clay. Then Adam made a fateful decision. He hired the wrong consultant; he listened to the voice of Satan rather than the voice of God and forfeited His moral likeness. Romans 5:12: "Sin entered the world through one man, and death through sin, and in this way death came to all men, because all sinned. . . ."

From that day on, the real hunger of the human heart has been for that lost image of God.

Appetites and Health

One sure sign of returning health is a restored appetite. Some time ago I underwent a major surgery to treat a tumor on the brain. Although the tumor was benign, the ordeal was grueling and left me wondering if life would ever be "normal" again. For weeks, nothing about my life seemed routine. But one day that changed. That was the day I suddenly stopped thinking about Pepto-Bismol and started thinking about pizza. My appetite had returned. It meant that I was getting well.

Healthy people have healthy appetites.

A healthy spiritual appetite is a sign of spiritual health, as well. We remember the day when our appetites changed from the pitiful appetizers of the world to the sumptuous entrées of the Kingdom. Through conversion, we were restored to spiritual health. As a result, our appetite for the things of God was restored.

David described that spiritual craving this way, "As the deer pants for streams of water, so my soul pants for you,

O God" (Ps. 42:1). Within the human heart, God implanted a hunger for companionship with Him. It is a hunger that will never be met in the mess halls of the world.

In this beatitude, Jesus shows that our search for righteousness cannot be a casual afterthought or hobby; it must be a way of life. Like the hunger pangs that make us desperate for food and the parched throat that makes us long for water, our souls must have a deep desire—a craving—for God.

The Appetite That Only God Can Appease

Among the interesting claims Jesus made about Himself are that He is the *Bread of Life* and the *Water of Life*. God intends to forever quench the spiritual appetites of His creation through the person of His Son, Jesus Christ. Every gift of grace and goodness comes from Him.

The pages of biblical history are dotted with signposts that lead directly to this Source.

In Matthew, He is the revelation of every prophecy.

In Mark, He is the savior of every sin.

In Luke, He is the healer of every hurt.

In John, He is the lord over every created thing.

In Acts, He is the name above every name.

In Romans, He is the lover of every outcast.

In First and Second Corinthians, He is the giver of every spiritual gift.

In Galatians, He is the liberator of every spiritual prisoner.

In Ephesians, He is the armor of every Christian soldier.

In Philippians, He is the author of every spiritual joy.

In Colossians, He is the ruler over every principality and power.

In First and Second Thessalonians, He is the sanctifier of every carnal heart.

In First and Second Timothy, He is the instructor of every Christian servant.

In Titus, He is the character of every church.

In Philemon, He is the brother of every slave.

In Hebrews, He is the perfecter of every saint.

In James, He is the respecter of every person.

In First and Second Peter, He is the encourager of every sufferer.

In John's letters, He is the lover of every soul.

In Jude, He is the keeper of every Christian.

In Revelation, He is the fulfillment of every promise.

Nineteenth-century Wesleyan songwriter Clara T. Williams acknowledged the fullness of His supply:

> All my lifelong I had panted
> > For a drink from some cool spring
> That I hoped would quench the burning
> > Of the thirst I felt within.
> Hallelujah! I have found Him—
> > Whom my soul so long has craved!
> Jesus satisfies my longings;
> > Thro' His blood I now am saved.

What's the message? We're not looking for something. We're looking for Someone.

Christ Is the Object of Our Search

In December 2001, "IT" finally arrived.

The gurus of gadgetry had been waiting in breathless wonder for the unveiling of "IT." The inventor of the heart stent, Dean Kamen, had promised a revolutionary invention. "IT" came just before Christmas.

What was it?

It was a high-tech, battery-powered transportation device called *Segway*. This two-wheeled people mover was designed to mimic the human body's ability to maintain its balance. It allowed riders to control speed and direction by shifting their weight and using a manual turning mechanism on one of the handlebars. It had a top speed of twelve miles per hour, and could go about fifteen miles on a single battery charge.

So that was it!

The tiresome months of speculation climaxed in the arrival of a machine designed to keep us from walking. It's likely that the news of this futuristic human transporter wasn't welcomed by a medical community already concerned about an under-exercised population.

If there were a spiritual Segway that could effortlessly transport people to God, it would be a hot seller. It would be advertised on the Internet, most likely, and some television shopping channel hostess would parade it in front of the cameras. It would be back ordered for weeks, no doubt. To a society looking for remote control righteousness and microwave mercy, a spiritual Segway would be just the thing.

Instant sanctification for an instant gratification society.

But God doesn't call us to an "it." He calls us to Himself through a decisive, dependent, and dedicated faith in the Lord Jesus Christ.

And the power that propels us toward Him doesn't come from a battery pack. It comes from the onboard presence of the Holy Spirit, who put motion to a gravestone in a Jerusalem cemetery and put life into the glorious Galilean lying in that borrowed tomb.

The songwriter didn't say, "Hallelujah! I have found *it*." Things don't fill the emptiness. She said, "Hallelujah! I have found *Him*." He is the end of our search.

Blessed (happy, contented) are those who find Him—for they shall be filled with Him.

But is the spiritual appetite quenched by one banquet—or is there a continual craving for the Christ?

A Continual Need

After supper, our first thought is usually this: "Now what?" After the last plate has been dish-washered, the last crumb Dirt-deviled, and the last leftover Tupper-wared, one thing remains: to plan the next meal. One breakfast, lunch, or dinner won't last a lifetime. Soon, another long day's work will be done, and a growling stomach will lecture us on the need to seek nourishment—again.

It's the same in the spiritual realm.

One meal does not suffice for a lifetime. I must have continual times of refreshment to satisfy my spiritual appetite. Acts 3:19: "Repent, then, and turn to God, so that your sins may be wiped out, that times of refreshing may come from the Lord. . . ." Notice that there will be *times* of refreshment, not a single repast.

The songwriter said it: "Morning by morning, new mercies I see. . . ."

Isaiah prophesied it:

> Come, all you who are thirsty,
>   come to the waters;
> and you who have no money,
>   come, buy and eat!
> Come, buy wine and milk
>   without money and without cost.
> Why spend money on what is not bread,
>   and your labor on what does not satisfy?
> Listen, listen to me, and eat what is good,
>   and your soul will delight in the richest of fare.
>   —Isaiah 55:1–2

Paul the apostle (and best-selling writer) fleshed it out in his own Christian experience. "Not that I have already obtained all this, or have already been made perfect, but I press on to take hold of that for which Christ Jesus took hold of me" (Phil. 3:12).

Selective Appetites

We human beings tend to be selective, even when we're hungry. Though the television program *Survivor* delighted in showing people eating bugs and worms, the trend never caught on in our finer restaurants. And though some cultures mean it when they say, "I'm so hungry, I could eat a horse," most of us would settle for a chicken sandwich. We're choosy about what we eat.

Sanctification is about selectivity, too.

Jesus says that those who have selective spiritual appetites will be blessed (happy, content). Only the intake of righteous things, and the right actions that result, will quench their appetites.

Happy are those who have an insatiable appetite for more of God.

Happy are those who will not settle for "carry out" commitment.

Happy are those who will take the time for a sit-down spiritual meal at the table of the Lord.

They will be filled!

It's said that in a lifetime, the average American will eat the equivalent of 150 cows, 225 lambs, 26 sheep, 310 hogs, 26 acres-worth of grain, and 50 acres-worth of fruit and vegetables. Yet the average Christian will try to satisfy spiritual hunger with only 365 Bible verses per year—or fewer.

The thriving Christians of the early church had a hunger and thirst for spiritual things. For example, when Christians in Berea went home from a preaching service, they got out their study Bibles and double-checked the sermon notes.

Acts 17:11: "Now the Bereans were of more noble character . . . for they received the message with great eagerness and examined the Scriptures every day to see if what Paul said was true."

We can do no less and expect to survive in these days of pluralistic religion. Some religious fare is not meat, but simply broth!

We need to be selective.

Real Satisfaction

"I'm stuffed," the well-fed diner declares with a push away from the table. That testimony proves the competency of the chef. The posture itself is evidence that the bill of fare was adequate to meet the diner's need.

The fourth beatitude doesn't promise me a spiritual soufflé. It promises solid food that will, as my grandmother used to say, "stick to your ribs." Jesus said that when you hunger and thirst for righteousness, you will be filled.

The longing that can be satisfied is your desire for God. When you hunger and thirst for righteousness, you will be filled.

Filled with what?

We Are Filled with Faith

If you hunger and thirst for God, He'll fill you with faith. First Corinthians 2:1–4: "When I came to you, brothers, I did not come with eloquence or superior wisdom as I proclaimed to you the testimony about God. For I resolved to know nothing while I was with you except Jesus Christ and him crucified. I came to you in weakness and fear, and with much trembling. My message and my preaching were not with wise and persuasive words, but with a demonstration of the Spirit's power, so that your faith might not rest on men's wisdom, but on God's power. . . ."

Paul recognized the source. He could only stand—and only have a good standing—through the merits and mercy of Christ. He was content because of his commitment.

We Are Filled with Purpose

If you hunger and thirst for God, He will fill you with purpose. A boatload of biblical fishermen made that discovery. Their bobbing and weaving on the fickle waves of Galilee became a love cruise on the ocean of God's purpose. Matthew 4:18–20:

> As Jesus was walking beside the Sea of Galilee, he saw two brothers, Simon called Peter and his brother Andrew. They were casting a net into the lake, for they were fishermen. "Come, follow me," Jesus said, "and I will make you fishers of men." At once they left their nets and followed him.

Dropping their "nots" in the sand, they picked up some "He shalls." Their lives acquired new meaning as they followed Jesus.

We Are Filled with Power

If you hunger and thirst for God, He will fill you with power. Paul was called to a ministry to the Gentiles that had batteries included. God said, "I am sending you to them to open their eyes and turn them from darkness to light, and from the power of Satan to God, so that they may receive forgiveness of sins and a place among those who are sanctified by faith in me" (Acts 26:17–18).

A sanctified heart isn't empty. It's filled with the Spirit of Christ.

When by faith we offer ourselves in total surrender to the will and purpose of God, He makes a great trade. He gives us not only enough cleansing to clear the last cobweb of rebellion from our hearts, but also enough equipping to carry out the very worst assignments! Acts 1:8: "But you will receive power when the Holy Spirit comes on you; and you will be my witnesses in Jerusalem, and in all Judea and Samaria, and to the ends of the earth."

Robert Murray McCheyne wrote a letter of congratulations to a young minister who was on his first assignment. In the letter, McCheyne included this advice, "In great measure, according to the purity and perfection of the instrument will be the success. It is not great talents God blesses so much as great likeness to Jesus. A holy minister is an awful weapon in the hand of God."

Blessed are those who hunger and thirst for righteousness, for they will be filled.

The fifth beatitude shows us how to put purity and power into practical use as we minister to the hurting.

CHAPTER 5

Blessed are the merciful,
for they will be shown mercy.
—Matthew 5:7

The word for mercy, as I understand it, comes from the combination of two Latin words, one meaning *heart*, the other *pity*. Mercy is God's undeserved and unhindered kindness. It sees the sin and suffering of the world and not only weeps but also moves to set free.

Mount Sinai, the mountain of the Ten Commandments, was a mountain of strict law, with hard-rock demands for regulation-weary travelers. The Mount of Beatitudes was a mountain of grace. Streams of mercy flowed there. Jesus later illustrated that mercy in answer to a disciple's question. Matthew 18:21–33:

> Then Peter came to Jesus and asked, "Lord, how many times shall I forgive my brother when he sins against me? Up to seven times?"

> Jesus answered, "I tell you, not seven times, but seventy-seven times.

> "Therefore, the kingdom of heaven is like a king who wanted to settle accounts with his servants. As he began the settlement, a man who owed him ten thousand talents was brought to him. Since he was not able to pay, the master ordered that he and his wife and his children and all that he had be sold to repay the debt.

"The servant fell on his knees before him. 'Be patient with me,' he begged, 'and I will pay back everything.' The servant's master took pity on him, canceled the debt and let him go.

"But when that servant went out, he found one of his fellow servants who owed him a hundred denarii. He grabbed him and began to choke him. 'Pay back what you owe me!' he demanded.

"His fellow servant fell to his knees and begged him, 'Be patient with me, and I will pay you back.'

"But he refused. Instead, he went off and had the man thrown into prison until he could pay the debt. When the other servants saw what had happened, they were greatly distressed and went and told their master everything that had happened.

"Then the master called the servant in. 'You wicked servant,' he said, 'I canceled all that debt of yours because you begged me to. Shouldn't you have had mercy on your fellow servant just as I had on you?'"

Blessed (happy, content) are those who practice forgiveness.

Someone said, "I wish doctors and lawyers didn't call what they do *practice*." Medical *practice*, law *practice*—it does have an interesting ring. After I've had all the blood tests, filled out the insurance papers and am ready for a major operation, I'd rather that the doctor wore a mask for some reason other than to cover his ignorance. Practice may make perfect, but you'd probably feel more comfortable if the attorney representing your interests had at least enough experience to know the judge from the court reporter.

But practice doesn't necessarily indicate a lack of inexperience. It may mean just the opposite.

The winning golf pro goes to the driving range and pulls the same club from the bag that she's used in countless tournaments. She addresses the ball just as her golf instructor advised years ago. Then begins the routine of *practice*. Time and again. Swing after swing. Day in and day out. The same stance. The same motion. The same concentration.

Practice.

Practice.

Practice.

It's the mark of a champion.

That kind of practice—customary action, habitual performance—makes a champion in the Kingdom as well as on the golf course.

So how can we "practice" this terrific truth? Let's put the parable on rewind. We can't miss a single point if we are to discover the blessedness of mercy and the contentment it brings.

Because We Are Forgiven

"The servant's master took pity on him, canceled the debt and let him go" (Matt. 18:27). The servant wasn't in a bargaining position. He had a debt he couldn't pay. In days of old, people who couldn't pay their debts weren't sent to a credit counseling agency. They were sent to prison! "Go directly to jail!" wasn't a cute idea for the corner position on a game board; it was a fact of life. Imprisoned and unable to work, the debtor was not the only one who suffered. His family paid as well. To owe a debt was a serious matter.

But Jesus faced some religious folk who believed they had no debt to pay. They assumed that they were in a bargaining position with God and bristled like a porcupine at the Master's pointed parable. John 8:31–33: "To the Jews who had believed him, Jesus said, 'If you hold to my teaching, you are really my disciples. Then you will know the truth, and the truth will set you free.' They answered him, 'We are Abraham's descendants and have never been slaves of anyone. How can you say that we shall be set free?'"

They failed to understand the enormity of their debt.

With surgical skill, the Great Physician made an incision directly to the heart of the matter. "Jesus replied, 'I tell you the truth, everyone who sins is a slave to sin. Now a slave has no permanent place in the family, but a son belongs to it forever. So if the Son sets you free, you will be free indeed" (John 8:34–36).

This amounted to more than a missed payment on a Visa bill. It was spiritual bankruptcy. The only way out was to be set free by Jesus, the Christ.

V. Gilbert Beers said, "Forgiveness is the balm of healing that soothes and heals the wounds of error." Elvina M. Hall put a face to that philosophy with a gospel song:

> Jesus paid it all;
>   All to Him I owe.
> Sin had left a crimson stain;
>   He washed it white as snow.

Until I know that I have been forgiven, I cannot know the happiness that comes from forgiving another. Ephesians 4:32: "Be kind and compassionate to one another, forgiving each other, just as in Christ God forgave you."

Not only is God merciful, He holds the patent on mercy. "Blessed be God, even the Father of our Lord Jesus Christ, the Father of mercies, and the God of all comfort . . ." (2 Cor. 1:3 KJV).

Robert Robinson wrote about that mercy in the great hymn, *Come Thou Fount of Every Blessing.*

Streams of mercy, never ceasing,
  Call for songs of loudest praise.
Teach me some melodious sonnet,
  Sung by flaming tongues above.
Praise the mount! I'm fixed upon it,
  Mount of God's unchanging love.

We freely forgive because we have been freely forgiven.

No Record of Wrongs

The unmerciful servant in Jesus' parable had dollar signs in his eyes. He grabbed a fellow slave and demanded ransom money. "Pay back what you owe me!" (Matt. 18:28). It's as if he pasted a barcode on the debtor's forehead and said, "This is the price of your freedom!"

There's a classic story of two sisters who had fought for most of their lives. As one lay on her deathbed, she asked for her "sparring partner." The sister came to the hospital room, where the gravely ill patient motioned for her to come near. As the patient pulled her sibling closer, she said softly, "Sister, you know there have always been problems between us. I want you to forgive me."

Her sister quickly responded, "It's alright, sister, I forgive you."

Then the patient's countenance changed and she said, "I also want you to know that if I make it through this, the war's still on!"

Who won that war? The sister who was willing to forgive, no matter the cost.

Forgiveness is free, but it's not inexpensive.

Jesus didn't price it out, however. He simply laid down His life. He relinquished His heavenly power and privilege to reconcile us to God. Ephesians 1:4–8:

For he chose us in him before the creation of the world to be holy and blameless in his sight. In love he predestined us to be adopted as his sons through Jesus Christ, in accordance with his pleasure and will—to the praise of his glorious grace, which he has freely given us in the One he loves. In him we have redemption through his blood, the forgiveness of sins, in accordance with the riches of God's grace that he lavished on us with all wisdom and understanding.

I heard the story of a judge who tried a young father accused of stealing groceries for his family at Christmastime. He listened to the young man's defense: "I can't find work, and my children are hungry." The judge debated the case in his mind for a few moments, then announced the sentence. He fined the man two hundred dollars plus court costs.

Heartless?

Here's the rest of the story. The next day, the judge drove to the young man's house with a van filled with groceries. "I can't believe it," said the astonished young father, helping the older man carry the groceries into the house.

The judge replied, "Young man, as a judge, I had an obligation to fine you. As a father, I wanted your family to have a merry Christmas."

God the righteous judge had an obligation to fine humanity for its sin—and the judgement was most severe: death. But the Son of Man became the eternal supply of our forgiveness. God the loving father wanted us to have a merry Christmas, so He stepped onto the front porch of our lives with the offering of His own Son.

That is the attitude of this beatitude.

Happy are those who are willing to pay any personal cost to win back the estranged—because they know that their own forgiveness has been purchased with just such an unlimited price.

Loss of pride.

Restitution.

"Crawling back."

Nothing on earth could equal the cost Christ was willing to pay for our forgiveness.

George Roemisch said, "Forgiveness is the fragrance of the violet which still clings fast to the heel that crushed it."

Blessed are the merciful . . .

Former president Ronald Reagan's daughter Patti wrote about his attitude after the 1982 attempt on his life: "The following day my father said he knew his physical healing was directly dependent on his ability to forgive John Hinckley."

. . . for they will be shown mercy.

Influence upon Others

"When the other servants saw what had happened, they were greatly distressed . . ." (Matt. 18:31). The only thing that might have changed the attitude of the bystanders toward the unmerciful servant was forgiveness.

Posturing.

Pay-off.

Fake wounds.

Sympathy.

None of these would change their minds. The unmerciful servant needed to cancel the debt instead of exacting it. Had he done so, the reaction of his peers would have been much different.

During a time of great civil unrest, Christians in Sierra Leone, West Africa, displayed forgiveness in a remarkable way. The rebel fighters in Sierra Leone's civil war were heartless. Hundreds of men, women, boys, and girls were maimed by these savage rebels. Many of the victims were Christians.

But instead of taking revenge, the Christians began to meet together for worship. Influenced by this display of forgiveness, some of the rebels began to attend the meetings, hearing the gospel message for the first time.

Forgiveness gets the attention of others—including our enemies.

It's interesting that in this high-decibel age, retail stores are able to market "sound machines," which do nothing but create noise. For a few dollars you can purchase your own brand of noise—anything from ocean waves to rushing wind, rain, or thunder. Just press "play," and the manufactured sound will drown out the noise around you.

Kenneth Chafin said, "Forgiveness isn't pretending nothing has happened, or pretending that what happened didn't hurt." In other words, forgiveness doesn't simply drown out the surrounding noise. Chafin adds, "Forgiveness is refusing to let anything permanently destroy the relationship." Forgiveness replaces the static of conflict with a sweeter sound.

That's what happened at Calvary.

Angry epithets filled the air like acrid smoke, choking those who wept on the rugged battleground where the sinless Son of God was dying. But soon a sweeter sound was heard above the din. Ever since, no one has been able to muffle it—not with warring words, and not with stinging criticism or demeaning put-downs. Luke 23:34: "Jesus said, 'Father, forgive them, for they do not know what they are doing.'"

It was the sound of forgiveness that echoed through the air.

Happy are those who drown out the angry noises of the world with words of forgiveness, for they will entice others to forgive.

The Canceled Debt

"In anger his master turned him over to the jailers to be tortured, until he should pay back all he owed" (Matt. 18:34). The master had no choice; the servant had to pay the debt or pay the penalty. There were laws to be kept. The master's own reputation was at stake. If he let this debtor off, others would default, and the law would become meaningless. Where there is no penalty, there is no law.

The unmerciful servant missed his chance. By withholding forgiveness, he missed the opportunity to be forgiven.

In the Old Testament, Israel's rebellion earned a wage of judgment—even annihilation. But judgment was mingled with mercy. Nehemiah 9:31: "In your great mercy you did not put an end to them or abandon them, for you are a gracious and merciful God."

Jesus explained why it is so important that mercy replace judgement. Luke 6:32–35:

> If you love those who love you, what credit is that to you? Even "sinners" love those who love them. . . . But love your enemies, do good to them, and lend to them without expecting to get anything back. Then your reward will be great, and you will be sons of the Most High, because he is kind to the ungrateful and wicked.

Jesus did more than just explain that concept. A short while later, He demonstrated it in a way that brought salvation to our guilt-ridden souls.

One Lord's day in Papua New Guinea, a group of missionaries gathered with local believers to observe the Lord's Supper. As one of the local young men sat down, he appeared to be very troubled. A missionary approached him and asked what was wrong. He said, "Do you see the man who just came in? He is the one who killed and cannibalized my father."

The air was thick with tension as the two men faced each other across the Lord's table—victim and victimizer; one aggrieved, the other repentant. Drawn breath was held in silence as the worshippers awaited the reaction of these sworn enemies.

After a few moments, the young man seemed to relax. The hard lines on his face softened, and he regained composure. He said to the missionary, "I did not know whether I could endure the pain and anger I had felt toward him because of the death of my father, but it is all right now. He is forgiven through the precious blood of our Lord, through which I too have found forgiveness."

Blessed are the merciful, for they will be shown mercy.

Does the condition of your heart affect your eyesight? Yes, according to the next beatitude.

CHAPTER 6

Blessed are the pure in heart, for they will see God.
—Matthew 5:8

D*ecision* magazine published a letter to Billy Graham that was written by a young girl. She asked, "How can I be good? I go to Sunday school and study the catechism, and I want to be good."

That is a basic question of human life: How can I be good?

How can I do what God wants me to do?

How can I be what God wants me to be?

How can I live a life that meets His requirements?

How can I be clean enough and holy enough to escape this prison of guilt that I feel?

In other words, if only the pure in heart are blessed and see God, how can I have a pure heart?

Some answer vehemently that it's impossible to have a pure heart. That, they imagine, is as ridiculous as telling a coal miner emerging from underground that his hands and face should be clean. It's a dirty world, we're told, and somebody has to live in it.

Here's another question: How pure is pure? Is there any wiggle room on holiness? Can I be *almost* pure before God?

In New York State a man was collecting sap from the sugar maples on his farm and boiling it into a maple syrup that was well known throughout the region. People traveled for miles to buy it. One day, some officials from the state government came and told him that he would have to stop selling syrup unless he changed the label.

They said, "Your label says '100% pure New York maple syrup.' But that can't be true. Nothing is one hundred percent pure."

Is there a problem with the labeling, or has God set an impossible standard? Is there any real-world hope for living above the tasteless tides of the times? Can I have a "pure heart"? And just how much purity do I need?

Enough, Jesus said, to see God. Enough purity to ensure an unobstructed view of His power, His provision, His forgiveness, His holiness, and His justice.

A Heart Problem

I watch as a large bird soars gracefully above a beautiful mountain meadow, held in midair by the warm summer currents. Gazing down upon the landscape, it spies something of interest. What could it be? Colorful wildflowers dance energetically in the summer breeze. Does it see them? No. The graceful limbs of a willow tree are doing hand motions to a midday lullaby. Could that be the object of interest? No. The elegant aviator watches something that interests it far more than these. It sees the carcass of an animal, rotting in the sun—fly-infested, maggot-filled, bloated.

How is that possible?

How could this creature focus on decaying waste while soaring above a field of dreams? Because it's a buzzard. It has a buzzard's appetite, a buzzard's eye view of reality, and a buzzard's heart. The buzzard in it obstructs its view of the beautiful and focuses on the grotesque.

What's the remedy?

That buzzard needs a change of heart so that it is free to focus on the pure instead of the putrid.

When there is a spiritual heart problem, it affects every facet of life—emotional, physical, and social. When the spiritual life flow is shut down, it prevents us from seeing God, from being connected to Him, from being blessed.

Guilt Causes "Heart Disease"

Guilt is at the cause of spiritual heart disease. It's the "plaque" that clogs the arteries of the spirit. One psychiatrist estimated that ninety percent of his patients could cure themselves if they could learn to deal with their guilt. Guilt is a prominent factor in our lives. Everyone has felt it, or will.

The dictionary defines guilt as "the act or state of having done a wrong or committed an offense." Guilt results from a willful act of disobedience against God. It produces guiltiness—a mournful attitude. The reason everyone feels guilt at some time or other is that everyone is guilty of disobeying God. The Bible says that "all have sinned and fall short of the glory of God" (Rom. 3:23).

Guilt isn't something that religion or medicine has invented to keep customers. It isn't a figment of the imagination that will go away if ignored. People *feel* guilty because they *are* guilty. And that guilt must be dealt with in several important ways.

It must be recognized.

It must be acknowledged.

It must be removed.

But how is that accomplished? Reams of paper and miles of audio- and videotape are filled with advice on dealing with guilt. What works?

Guilt before Grace

Guilt can be removed, and must be, but it does serve a useful purpose. Just as physical pain can be the motivator that drives a person to seek medical treatment, so guilt is the prod that moves us toward a right relationship with God.

In the early days of the Methodist movement, particularly in the camp meetings, there was an item called the *Mourners' Bench*. It was a long, rough wooden bench at the front of the meeting place. At the invitation of the speaker, people would come forward and kneel at the bench to weep and mourn, expressing sorrow for their sin.

What makes people weep over their sin? It's the *conviction* brought by the Holy Spirit, reminding them that they have exceeded God's speed limit.

When you feel guilty, make a traffic stop. Use it as an occasion to examine your heart.

To remove guilt, you must acknowledge its source: sin. Only when you have confessed your sin before God can guilt be removed. Only then are you ready for a pure heart.

The Satisfying Source

Ponce de León wandered the Florida swamps searching for the fountain of youth. He never found it. Those who search for the source of holiness face no such disappointment. Christ is the Source, and you can drink from this fountain at any time.

Surrender to God

First, however, you must recognize that you cannot make yourself righteous. In human relationships, restoration and forgiveness must come from the one who has been wronged.

Spiritual forgiveness and restoration must come from the one against whom we have sinned.

Ultimately, all sin is sin against God because it is God's law that has been broken. And the only way to find forgiveness is by agreeing with Him about your guilt. If you'll take one step toward Him, He'll take two. He'll forgive. He'll cover the sadness of your sin with the goodness of His grace. He has guaranteed that outcome by the death of His only son, the Lord Jesus Christ.

The result of your repentance and faith is forgiveness, the beginning of holiness. The Apostle Paul said in Romans 8:1, "Therefore, there is now no condemnation for those who are in Christ Jesus. . . ."

That means no guilt.

One man responded to my altar invitation to receive Christ as his Savior. He confessed his sin and was forgiven. He said, "I felt as though a heavy bundle that I have carried around for years has just rolled off my back."

The load of guilt was gone.

Seek Cleansing

After receiving forgiveness, we still need to be purified. Even Paul, an apostle of Jesus Christ, acknowledged that there was a glitch remaining on the hard drive of his heart. He said:

> I know that nothing good lives in me, that is, in my sinful nature. For I have the desire to do what is good, but I cannot carry it out. . . .
>
> Who will rescue me from this body of death? (Rom. 7:18, 24).

He then answered his own question with this boisterous affirmation: "Thanks be to God—through Jesus Christ our Lord!" (Rom. 7:25). In other words, there is a solution to this problem, and His name is Jesus! That's why John promised, "If we confess our sins, he is faithful and just and will forgive us our sins and *purify us from all unrighteousness*" (1 John 1:9, emphasis added).

Cleansing follows forgiveness.

The Pure Heart

There is a word in the Bible that refers to the Holy Spirit's purifying work. That word is *sanctification.* Some folk are confused and some are troubled over its use, but they needn't be. *Sanctification* is a good, New Testament word. In fact, the Bible says "it is God's will that you should be sanctified" (1 Thess. 4:3a).

Sanctification, as it is used in the Bible, has a dual meaning.

Holy Means Set Apart

In its earliest and simplest use, sanctification referred to being set apart for a holy purpose. For example, the Tabernacle and, later, the Temple were *sanctified*: they were set aside for a special purpose. They were used exclusively as places of worship. They were holy.

In that sense, speaking of His disciples, Jesus said, "For them I sanctify myself, that they too may be truly sanctified" (John 17:19). In other words, I separate myself for a holy purpose (death on the Cross) so that my disciples may themselves be separated for a holy purpose.

That provision is not limited to the disciples of Jesus' day.

All Christians are sanctified, in that they are separated from the world as holy people—people dedicated to the Lord. Jesus said of His followers, "They are not of the world, even as I am not of it" (John 17:16). He didn't mean that they were, literally, taken out of the world, but that they would be different from the world.

Holy Means Pure

There is a second, and perhaps deeper, meaning of the word *sanctification*. It not only means set apart for a holy use, but it also means *made pure*.

The little girl asked, "How can I be good?" The answer is that she can't, not by her own ingenuity.

All of the good works done by people in the name of humanity, government, or even Church, leave their doers like Lady MacBeth, vainly scrubbing her hands in an effort to be rid of the incriminating stain of her crime. The stain of sin can only be washed away by the cleansing power of the blood of Christ, through the indwelling of God's Holy Spirit.

Many people get this backwards.

They try to be good or do good things so God will recognize their holiness. But good works never produce holiness. It is holiness of heart that produces good works. If your heart is holy, your thoughts and actions will be holy (Gal. 5:22–23).

Yet when we confess our sin to God, we are forgiven; and when we consecrate ourselves fully to God, the Holy Spirit brings cleansing to our hearts.

Blessed are the pure in heart.

They Shall See God

An unobstructed view of God is a remedy for failing faith. Paul said, "I pray also that the eyes of your heart may be enlightened in order that you may know the hope to which he has called you, the riches of his glorious inheritance in the saints, and his incomparably great power for us who believe. That power is like the working of his mighty strength, which he exerted in Christ when he raised him from the dead and seated him at his right hand in the heavenly realms . . ." (Eph. 1:18–20).

The pure in heart have an unobstructed view of the Creator.

They See the Majesty of God

September 11, 2001, is a day that, to borrow the words of President Roosevelt, "will live in infamy." For the rest of my life I will remember where I was and what I was doing that morning when a suicide squad of terrorist flew jet airliners loaded with tons of highly flammable fuel into the twin towers of New York's World Trade Center.

Time seemed to move in slow motion.

A horrified nation wept and watched in disbelief as those monuments of architectural strength and economic power crumbled in a choking, billowing cloud of dust. Along with them, at least eight nearby buildings either fell or were damaged beyond repair.

Surprisingly, St. Paul's Chapel, located directly across the street from the World Trade Center, stood untouched by the devastation. The two-hundred-thirty-year-old church was coated with a layer of dust, but was otherwise unharmed amid the wreckage.

Mayor Rudolph Guliani called it a miracle.

Immediately, the old house of worship became a "city of refuge," where the suffering, searching, battered, bewildered victims and their rescuers gathered. Amidst the destruction, they discovered hope. In the face of fear, they found solace.

On that battlefield of horror, God, in His sovereign compassion, had already raised a symbol of hope. At the very epicenter of man's evil, we saw the holiness of God.

They See the Mercy of God

Mark 16:9: "When Jesus rose early on the first day of the week, he appeared first to Mary Magdalene, out of whom he had driven seven demons." Mary was a well-to-do woman whose life was filled with privilege but was tormented by demon possession. Jesus not only cured her heart, He gave her eyes to see one of the greatest sights in history: the Resurrection. In the rigid patriarchal society of Bible times, His post-resurrection revelation to her was nothing short of magnificent mercy.

Blessed are those whose hearts are pure enough to understand that God is not prejudiced by who we are or what we have.

They See the Mission of God

Seven centuries before the birth of Christ, the prophet Isaiah recorded this vision:

> In the year that King Uzziah died, I saw the Lord seated on a throne, high and exalted, and the train of his robe filled the temple. Above him were seraphs, each with six wings: With two wings they covered their faces, with two they covered their feet, and with two they were flying. And they were calling to one another:
>
> > "Holy, holy, holy is the Lord Almighty;
> > the whole earth is full of his glory."
>
> . . . Then I heard the voice of the Lord saying, "Whom shall I send? And who will go for us?"
>
> And I said, "Here am I. Send me!" (Isa. 6:1–3, 8).

Blessed are those whose hearts are pure enough to envision their role in the revival of their land.

20/20 Vision

The pure in heart have corrected vision. The change of heart affects their eyesight. They see God clearly for the first time. That enables them to see the world—and their place in it—with a proper focus. The results are life changing.

As a pastor I was asked to conduct a funeral for a homeless man in my community. "There probably won't be anyone in attendance," the funeral director advised, and he was right. Other than myself, the only people who came were the funeral home employees.

Yet to my surprise, the guest book outside at the chapel was filled with names. "I thought this man had no friends," I said. "Where did all these names come from?"

The funeral director explained. "Yesterday there was another funeral across the hall. It was for the father of a teenage girl from my church. When this girl found out that the homeless fellow had no friends, she asked everyone who signed her father's guest book to sign his book as well."

That young lady saw hope in hopelessness and purpose in pain. She saw a way to serve others though suffering herself. She saw God.

Blessed are the pure in heart.

The next beatitude examines the traits of a rather prominent family—the Family of God.

CHAPTER 7

Blessed are the peacemakers,
for they will be called sons of God.
—Matthew 5:9

God has a family album. And just like earthly photo albums that capture a variety of human characteristics on Kodak paper or in Microsoft files, God's album displays a variety of spiritual characteristics. One trait is predominant. It is seen on the face of every child in God's family.

That trait is peace.

Peace is in the spiritual DNA of the child of God. The head of the family is called the Prince of Peace, and those who exhibit the family resemblance by making peace are called sons of God.

We live in a world that talks as much about peace as it does the weather—and with as little effect. In spite of our many so-called solutions contrived by social scientists of renown, we usually end up making war instead of peace. We're like the unfortunate firefighters who were called to rescue a cat that was stuck in a tree. Their rescue was successful—carried out to the last jot and tittle of the department manual. But as the firefighters put their truck in gear to return to the station, they backed over the same animal that they had just rescued.

They had the right motive, but they ended up with the wrong result!

Blessed (happy, content) are the peacemakers—those who have learned to translate their good intentions into lasting peace.

Happy People

In a world at war, there are those who have learned the secret of peace. They are peacemakers, and they have discovered the way to be at peace in a world at war. Scripture tells us how.

They've Gone to the Right Source

I've learned that I must experience peace in my own heart before I can express it in the world.

There was a frightened soldier who was running from sniper bullets. He dove into a bunker, thinking that he was alone. To his surprise, another solder crawled over beside him. The second soldier happened to be wearing a cross pendant.

"Thank goodness you're here!" the frightened private exclaimed. And pointing to a cross around the other fellow's neck, he asked, "How do you work that thing, anyway?"

The Cross of Christ isn't something we "work." It is, rather, something that works *for us*. Amid the bitter political and religious wrangling on Golgotha's hill, our peace agreement with God was forever settled. Jesus Christ was both the arbitrator and the offering. ·

> For he himself is our peace, who has made the two one and has destroyed the barrier, the dividing wall of hostility, by abolishing in his flesh the law with its commandments and regulations. His purpose was to create in himself one new man out of the two, thus making peace, and in this one body to reconcile both of them to God through the

cross, by which he put to death their hostility. He came and preached peace to you who were far away and peace to those who were near. For through him we both have access to the Father by one Spirit (Eph. 2:14–18).

You can have more crosses around your neck than a busload of rock stars and still not be related to Christ—or enjoy the benefit of His peace in your heart. The Bible says that peace is one of the fruits of the Spirit—a by-product of faith in Christ.

Jesus is the peace source.

They've Made the Right Connection

Old Testament prophets knew the secret of peacemaking: prayer. Psalm 122:6: "Pray for the peace of Jerusalem: May those who love you be secure."

Where does security come from? It comes in answer to prayer!

The prophets made the right connection. As a matter of fact, it takes extra effort to be at war with someone on your prayer list.

Why should prayer be a last resort rather than a first response?

Sometimes we're like the little boy who wanted a new CD player for Christmas. He said to his parents, "I just don't know what to do. I don't know whether to ask Santa, or pray for it." Someone wrote, "Prayer is not a device for getting our will done through heaven but a desire that God's will would be done on earth through us."

In that prayer we know as the Lord's Prayer, Jesus taught inquiring disciples the perfect beginning for every petition. "Our Father in heaven, hallowed be your name, your kingdom come, your will be done on earth as it is in heaven" (Matt. 6:9–10). At the core of every effective spiritual request is acquiescence to the will of God.

Peace *there* makes peace *everywhere*.

Peacemakers are happy because they're connected to God through prayer.

They've Taken the Right Step

Unresolved issues are like unplayed melodies—the tune exists, but nobody has any fun until the music starts. In relationships, problem resolution is music to the ears.

Jesus reminded us that when we kneel to pray and remember that someone has a "two-car grudge" against us, we should go and make the wrongs right. One sage said, "Many people mean well, but their meanness is worse than their wellness."

The seventh beatitude is about taking the first step.

Romans 12:18: "If it is possible, as far as it depends on you, live at peace with everyone." Simply put, if you want to be a peacemaker, tear down your half of the fence. What an influence that would be upon a war-weary world!

When my youngest son was in the second grade, his school was located along my route to work. That allowed me a wonderful opportunity to spend time with him each day. Every morning the two of us would have breakfast together, and I would drop him off at school on my way to the office. We enacted the same ritual each day. Just before my son opened the car door, I would lean over and give him a kiss, saying, "I love you, Bud." He would respond, "I love you too, Dad."

One day, everything changed.

As we arrived at the school, my son noticed a group of his friends waiting for him on the sidewalk. As I leaned over to give him a kiss, he suddenly thrust out his arm and asked, "Couldn't we just shake hands today?"

I longed to wrap my arms around him in a father's loving embrace, but of course, I respected his wishes.

The next day, I held my hand for shake when to my surprise my son leaned over for the customary kiss. "It's OK, Dad," he explained, "I've thought it over."

Sons of God think it over. And they come to the conclusion that the opinions of the crowd are less important than the affirmation of the Father.

Sons of God initiate peace first in their own attitudes.

If you dwell on peace in your mind, it will break out in your actions. Luke 6:45: "The good man brings good things out of the good stored up in his heart, and the evil man brings evil things out of the evil stored up in his heart. For out of the overflow of his heart his mouth speaks."

But attitude alone won't make peace. It must become an *action*. Peace is a practice, not just a principle. Peacemakers make peace just as piano players play the piano. They write that letter of apology, make that conciliatory phone call, send that E-mail of reconciliation. They have their cup of coffee along with a piece of "humble pie."

Peacemaking seems awkward at first. You may feel like the little girl who wrote a letter to God: "Dear God, I just started taking violin lessons, so don't listen. I still squeak a lot." But soon, the awkwardness will fade, and peacemaking will come naturally.

Actively.

Humbly.

Immediately.

Seek peace. It's the right step. Take it and be blessed.

They Follow the Right Example

Someone wrote of Jesus, "He loves us before we respond, he forgives us before we ask, and blesses us when we are undeserving." That's an accurate description of the Master. That's the example we follow.

I heard the amazing story of eleven people who found themselves adrift on an ice flow that was headed for a waterfall. The brother of one stranded person arrived at the scene and begged gawking bystanders to mount a rescue. They refused. He offered money. They still refused. "It's too dangerous," they concluded.

So the brother took this desperate step: he tied a line around his waist, waded into the water, and invited others to do the same. Four of the onlookers responded, forming a human chain. Inching their way into the cold water, they achieved what money couldn't buy—the rescue of every person trapped on the ice.

Christ offered His own life as an example. He offered Himself as the rescuer, and then said to a watching world, "Tie yourself to me." Together with Him, we can reach those trapped in conflict. We can make peace.

Seeing the beauty of Christ's example, we must respond. We must tie ourselves to Him, embracing the peace that He offered through His death. We must acknowledge with the Apostle Paul, "All this is from God, who reconciled us to himself through Christ and gave us the ministry of reconciliation . . ." (2 Cor. 5:18).

Peacemakers are happy; they know that they follow the right example.

Children of God

Jesus said, "Blessed are the peacemakers, for they shall be called sons of God." What an honor!

Have you ever wondered why our relationship with God is compared to the relationship between a father and son? The Apostle Paul said, "For you did not receive a spirit that makes you a slave again to fear, but you received the Spirit of sonship. And by him we cry, '*Abba*, Father'" (Rom. 8:15). And John said, "How great is the love the Father has lavished on us, that we should be called children of God! And that is what we are!" (1 John 3:1).

For many, the implications of that relationship are lost in life's shuffle.

Thousands of sons and daughters don't understand the love that can exist between a father and his children. It's sad that many people miss the joy of knowing their earthly fathers, but even sadder is that millions more do not know the joy of being children of God. Peacemakers are children of God.

That relationship affords unique privileges.

The Father Approves of His Children

Our heavenly Father doesn't make excuses for us. He is too holy to do that. But He does approve of us—from the curl of our hair to the turn of our toes. He has signed-off on us. Genesis 1:31: "God saw all that he had made, and it was very good."

Biometrics is a twenty-first century industry that has become increasingly necessary. It is the science of identifying people by means of their biological traits. These unique characteristics are measured and recorded via retina scans, fingerprinting, and other methods. Comparisons of this data to computer stores of information on known criminals can alert security personnel to a potential problem.

In Christ, you and I have passed through the security cameras of heaven and have been accepted! David sang the Father's acceptance in a song that should embarrass every purveyor of positive thinking by comparison.

> My frame was not hidden from you
>> when I was made in the secret place.
> When I was woven together in the depths of the earth,

your eyes saw my unformed body.
All the days ordained for me
were written in your book
before one of them came to be.
—Psalm. 139:15–16

"Happy are the peacemakers," Jesus said, because they know their father, and He welcomes them.

The Father Provides for His Children

Jesus said it plainly: God's children have no need to worry. Matthew 6:31-32: "So do not worry, saying, 'What shall we eat?' or 'What shall we drink?' or 'What shall we wear?' . . . Your heavenly Father knows that you need them."

Food.

Clothing.

Shelter.

Transportation.

Employment.

He knows.

Happiness is knowing that your Father will take care of you. Our heavenly Father knows our need and has promised to meet it. That goes for tomorrow as well as today.

And, as a father, He can distinguish between our needs and wants. Our "wish list" may not match heaven's delivery ticket. Occasionally, earthly fathers say no. A child may present a reasonable request (reasonable to the child, anyway!) for the one thing that will make him or her "the happiest person in the world."

"But Dad, everybody has one!"

"But Dad, all the kids are doing it!"

Yet a loving father exercises judgment. He knows that sometimes a granted request will bring more harm than good. So, he says "No." Or, "Not now."

Has God ever refused your request? You asked for health, wealth, position, or something you believed was in your best interest, and God didn't supply it.

Sad day? No.

Glad day!

You're His child. Father knows what you need, and He is supplying it in ways you don't understand.

The Father Forgives His Children

One of the greatest character portrayals in the Bible is that of the Prodigal Son's father. When his son insisted on settling the estate, the father gave him his share. When the son gathered his belongings and took that fateful journey to a far country—the "Siberia of the soul"—the father let him go.

Heartbreaking!

This man knew that his son was headed the wrong way. He knew, perhaps from experience, the heartache that lay at the road's dead end. But he embraced his son, then stood at the gate, watching him go.

Perhaps you are the child in that journey. You wouldn't be the first, nor will you be the last, to say no to God and go your own way.

But the story has a happy ending.

The Prodigal returned. "I will arise and go to my father," he decided. "I will own up to my disobedience."

Jesus said, "So he got up and went to his father. But while he was still a long way off, his father saw him and was filled with compassion for him; he ran to his son, threw his arms around him and kissed him" (Luke 15:20).

Love's embrace proved stronger than the world's tug. There was comfort at home, and he knew it. There was forgiveness there, and he felt it deep within his heart.

Happiness is knowing a heavenly Father who waits by the gate—a Father who waits to forgive.

Getting It Right

It was one of those church bulletin announcements that went awry. In a section reserved for prayer requests, I noticed that a word had been left out. It read, "Please pray for a young father of four who needs to get life right." If the editor had to do over again, the word "his" might have been added. As it is, it's an interesting reminder—all of us need to get life right.

We only have one life; we must live it right the very first time. That's why making peace with God and others must be a priority. Peacemaking is the secret to contentment; it is the essence of sonship.

Blessed are you, peacemaker. You are a child of God.

Happy in a hail storm? The next beatitude tells us how we can be content even when people throw stones at us!

CHAPTER 8

Blessed are those who are persecuted because of righteousness,
for theirs is the kingdom of heaven.

—Matthew 5:10

A t first, the eighth beatitude seems paradoxical. Blessed
are those who are persecuted? That's like saying,
"Happy are those who get punched in the nose!"
Jesus made an interesting promise to His followers:
"Sooner or later, you're going to take a punch in the nose."
That's not a direct quote, but it conveys the message of John
16:32–33.

> "But a time is coming, and has come, when you will be
> scattered, each to his own home. You will leave me all
> alone. Yet I am not alone, for my Father is with me.
>
> "I have told you these things, so that in me you may
> have peace. In this world you will have trouble. But take
> heart! I have overcome the world."

In this world you will have trouble. That wouldn't make a
very good commercial for Christianity. Most advertisements
don't play up the fine print. The big splash is not about the
limited warranty or the "no returns" policy.

The community service organization doesn't say, "Join us
and stand on a street corner in sub-zero weather with a plastic bucket in your hand." No, they don't say it, but anyone
who joins a service organization expects it.

Why?

They've seen others standing on street corners in sub-zero

weather with plastic buckets in their hands! They understand that a few inconveniences are commingled with the incentives for doing good.

It's no different in the Kingdom. Signup, and you'll endure a few sub-zero days. But along with that inconvenience, there will be rich rewards.

Hassles Guaranteed

From the first eventful days in the Garden of Eden until now, it has been obvious that not everyone is a friend to those who are friends with God.

Jeremiah the prophet discovered that, making mud balls in a well.

Daniel the devout pray-er discovered that, trying to get comfortable in a lion cage.

Mary the mother of Jesus discovered that, reading the gossip column in the Nazareth News.

Peter the apostle discovered that, hanging upside down on an executioner's cross.

John the revelator discovered that, sending messages in a bottle from the isle of Patmos.

John Wesley the revivalist discovered that, dodging rocks on an open-air platform.

John Hus the apologist discovered that, while flames of martyrdom seared his skin.

Corrie Ten Boom, the "Tramp for the Lord," discovered that, gasping for air in the boxcar of a Nazi prison train.

Dayna Curry and Heather Mercer, Christian aid workers, discovered that, fighting the cold of a Kabul jail cell.

Jesus never promised that we would live our days without adversity. He did promise that we would never face a day without His presence. He vowed publicly that when we walk the dimly lit alleyways of life, He will be at our side.

Persecution has been the constant companion of Christ's church. Before the cake had been cut at the first birthday celebration, its members were dodging the arrows of opposition. More familiar to its leaders than the amenities of a luxury suite were the damp, dark, and utter loneliness of a dungeon. Then, as now, to raise a banner of allegiance to the Galilean was to invite enemy fire.

Happy in Persecution

But Jesus said, "Blessed are those who are persecuted," meaning that they are happy or content. There must be a reason for that. Scripture shows that there are reasons to be happy even when we are ill used by others.

We Know That God Allows Persecution

The fact that persecution exists didn't come as a celestial surprise. The all-seeing, all-knowing Designer wrote it into the specs for life's master plan. Persecution wasn't a last-minute add-on. It's there by design.

David reminds us, "Your eyes saw my unformed body. All the days ordained for me were written in your book before one of them came to be" (Ps. 139:16). Unlike earthly parents, the heavenly Father filled in the pages of our baby book even before we saw the light of day. And not all of those pages have pretty pink trim. Some are framed in gray and are tear-stained.

Did God delight in adding adversity to our itinerary? Yes, but not in some macabre way. The Bible says that His thoughts are not the same as ours. Though our adversity breaks His heart in a way no earthly father could understand, He delights in working His sovereign purpose through us.

There are no folding chairs in heaven; it's a busy place. If its messengers aren't making preparations for an eternal celebration, they're rushing to the crime scenes of life to assist victims—including us. But there's a difference between Rescue One and God's relief agency. God doesn't need a police scanner to find out where the trouble is. He's on the scene at all times, in full control.

Satan, the enemy of our faith, must meekly approach the Lord of heaven for permission before he can lift a finger against us. The Old Testament figure Job made that discovery. Job 1:8–12:

> Then the Lord said to Satan, "Have you considered my servant Job? There is no one on earth like him; he is blameless and upright, a man who fears God and shuns evil."

> "Does Job fear God for nothing?" Satan replied. "Have you not put a hedge around him and his household and everything he has? You have blessed the work of his hands, so that his flocks and herds are spread throughout the land. But stretch out your hand and strike everything he has, and he will surely curse you to your face."

> The Lord said to Satan, "Very well, then, everything he has is in your hands, but on the man himself do not lay a finger."

Did God know about Job's pending holocaust?
Of course!
Did He approve it?
Yes, to accomplish His sovereign purpose. Absolutely nothing happens without the knowing nod of earth's Creator. He is Lord not only over the *pinnacles* of life, but also over the *pits!*

Earth's worst can do their best to wring the joy out of your heart, but you can still be blessed (happy, content) because both *anything* and *everything* fall within the parameters of God's will.

We Know That Persecution Has Limits

There are limits to what Satan can do. Job understood that principle also; he learned it during a hurricane.

That's when God asked one of those "father questions"—you know the type, those that already have an answer. In Job 38:8–11 God asked: "Who shut up the sea behind doors when it burst forth from the womb, when I made the clouds its garment and wrapped it in thick darkness, when I fixed limits for it and set its doors and bars in place, when I said, 'This far you may come and no farther; here is where your proud waves halt?"

Can we be content in a crisis?

Yes.

I made the discovery in a first-person way. Facing a life-threatening surgery and painful recovery, I discovered that a crisis cannot control the Christ. He says to calamity: "This far you may come and no farther."

Heaven paints the sidelines in the game of life. And the Referee of all time tells Calamity when it is out of bounds—remember those waves on Galilee?

Paul said, "No temptation has seized you except what is common to man. And God is faithful; he will not let you be tempted beyond what you can bear. But when you are tempted, he will also provide a way out so that you can stand up under it" (1 Cor. 10:13). James added, "Blessed is the man who perseveres under trial, because when he has stood the test, he will receive the crown of life that God has promised to those who love him. When tempted, no one should say, 'God is tempting me.' For God cannot be tempted by evil, nor does he tempt anyone . . ." (James 1:12–13).

Blessed is the one who perseveres.

Where?

Down here on the playing field, not in the stands.

We Know That Persecution is Meaningful

When you are persecuted it shows that you belong to Jesus Christ. Jesus said we would suffer because of Him. In fact, when we suffer we are following in His footsteps. John 1:11–12: "He came to that which was his own, but his own did not receive him. Yet to all who received him, to those who believed in his name, he gave the right to become children of God. . . ."

The fact that hell's troops are arrayed against you is a sign that you're on the right side—God's side. You belong to Him. Consequently, you take the heat—the rebellion and revenge that are focused on Him and ricochet to you.

But you also have the honor.

Ephesians 2:6: "And God raised us up with Christ and seated us with him in the heavenly realms in Christ Jesus. . . ."

He has "seated us with him."

Persecution simply enhances our position. Every crisis moves us a notch up on the corporate ladder of heaven. Our happiness doesn't come from our triumph over trials; it comes from the fact that we belong to Jesus Christ. Even at the lowest moment in our lives, we are in an "exalted position" through faith in Him.

Enduring persecution also marks our membership in a great fraternity—the fellowship of the faithful. "In the same way they persecuted the prophets who were before you." When you walk through the valley of the shadow, you aren't just part of the team, you're in the hall of fame! Read Hebrews 11:17–40, and you'll see that the persecuted are in pretty good company.

Abraham.

Isaac.
Jacob.
David.
Gideon.

Persecution puts you in the ballpark with Scripture stand-outs who discovered purpose in their pain. What you suffer has meaning. That's reason to rejoice.

Theirs Is the Kingdom

I can be happy in persecution because I know that it affects me only here, where I am now, and not where I'm going. Abraham's family knew that. "By faith he made his home in the promised land like a stranger in a foreign country; he lived in tents, as did Isaac and Jacob, who were heirs with him of the same promise. For he was looking forward to the city with foundations, whose architect and builder is God" (Heb. 11:9–10).

In our hearts we know that we have a different post office box. We are citizens of a spiritual Kingdom.

It Is a Kingdom on Earth

When we were born spiritually into God's family, we became citizens of His Kingdom. You may live in the East, the West, the North, or the South. You may live on the Australian, African, or Asian continent. You may have voting privileges in North America, or you may have a summer home in South America. But by faith in the Lord Jesus Christ, you are first and foremost a citizen of His Kingdom.

Here and now.

It's a kingdom with a supreme authority. Jesus Christ is the king—the head of all principalities and powers. He is the sovereign ruler of the Kingdom of Heaven on earth. He has veto power over every kingdom decision. He is responsible for the health, wealth, and welfare of every citizen.

It's a kingdom with its own constitution. The Word of God, the Bible, is its code. It will never be amended, and it is never outdated. Its author is the Holy Spirit. Its message was breathed into the minds and hearts of forty writers who faultlessly transcribed every sacred word.

It's a kingdom with its own support system. Its citizens invite others into the kingdom, then encourage, correct, work beside, and laugh and cry with one another.

They open their fellowship to others.

They reach out in forgiveness.

They instruct with patience.

They love unconditionally.

God has given the persecuted a society that will not fail or forsake them. Throughout time, that community has joined hands in the arena, facing the ravages of wild beasts. It has offered its talents to bring cure and comfort to the hurting and hopeless. It has taught its young to love God first, and then others. It has proclaimed and practiced holiness amid immorality and opposition. It has shown armies the way to lay down arms and make peace.

It is the spiritual kingdom of the eternal God that is real, here and now.

It Is a Kingdom Yet to Come

Children of God travel the earth on a temporary visa. Their true home is in another place. They are citizens of earth but heirs to heaven—a kingdom that is to come. Somewhere, out there, God has built an eternal dwelling that is free from the trials of time.

Free from setbacks.

Free from suffering

Free from sadness.

God has a place for us, and He wants nothing more than to "put us in our place." It's His final prize for faithfulness, the ultimate trophy for endurance.

Until then?

We persevere. Hebrews 10:32–36:

Remember those earlier days after you had received the light, when you stood your ground in a great contest in the face of suffering. Sometimes you were publicly exposed to insult and persecution; at other times you stood side by side with those who were so treated. You sympathized with those in prison and joyfully accepted the confiscation of your property, because you knew that you yourselves had better and lasting possessions.

So do not throw away your confidence; it will be richly rewarded. You need to persevere so that when you have done the will of God, you will receive what he has promised.

The news report told of a woman named Kelly Perkins, who climbed the 19,340-foot elevation of Mount Kilimanjaro. Many others had climbed the mountain, the highest in Africa. What was different about this climber?

The difference was that Kelly was a heart patient. More than that, she was a heart *transplant* patient. Six years after her surgery, she made the climb to prove that people who have a new heart can be high achievers.

It wasn't easy.

Climbing in twenty-degree-below-zero weather, sometimes knocked to the ground by gusting winds, Kelly moved slowly toward the summit. Her fellow climbers had to stop. The journey was too grueling for them. But Kelly kept going. Each day for seven days she climbed, inching her way along the forty-five mile ascent.

And she made it.

After the climb, a television reporter interviewed Kelly and asked whether she was afraid. Her answer was almost as dramatic as her climb. She said, "I'm not afraid of dying. I'm most afraid of not really living."

Eight beatitudes show us how to really live.

Jesus' words are aimed at those who stand at the base of life's mountain and those who are mid-way to the top. To timid travelers afraid of living and to weary climbers afraid of dying, heaven shouts this encouragement:

Blessed are the poor in spirit,
 for theirs is the kingdom of heaven.
Blessed are those who mourn,
 for they will be comforted.
Blessed are the meek,
 for they will inherit the earth.
Blessed are those who hunger and thirst for righteousness,
 for they will be filled.
Blessed are the merciful,
 for they will be shown mercy.
Blessed are the pure in heart,
 for they will see God.
Blessed are the peacemakers,
 for they will be called sons of God.
Blessed are those who are persecuted because of righteousness,
 for theirs is the kingdom of heaven.

And blessed are you, weary pilgrim, as you live on earth and dream of heaven. Take these words to your heart, and keep climbing.